SECOND SKIN

Everyday and Sacred Uses of Bark Worldwide

ROYAL ALBERT MEMORIAL MUSEUM & ART GALLERY EXETER

Published in January 2004

ISBN: 185522-903-X

Text by Len Pole, Sherry Doyal,
with contributions by Jane Burkinshaw.

Photographs by David Garner
Design by Henry Lyndsay
Printed by Acanthus

The Royal Albert Memorial Museum & Art Gallery
Exeter wishes to acknowledge the financial support it
has received from the Designation Challenge Fund,
operated through Resource and the Department of
Culture Media and Sport, in the preparation and
publication of this catalogue.

Len Pole is Curator of Ethnography and Collections &
Interpretation Officer at the Royal Albert Memorial
Museum & Art Gallery.

Sherry Doyal is a freelance plant materials conservator.

Jane Burkinshaw is Assistant Curator of Ethnography at
the Royal Albert Memorial Museum & Art Gallery.

Exeter City Council

Foreword

Our main aim in this catalogue is to demonstrate the multifarious uses of bark and show the amazing number of barkcloth designs which have been produced in the last 250 years by artists both known and unknown. This can be achieved in the Exeter museum because, since its foundation in the 1860s, many examples of objects made of bark and barkcloth from many parts of the world have been acquired, mostly by donation. Over 100 are illustrated in this catalogue. Most of these examples were acquired by their original collectors because they combined in an easily portable form the exotic and the familiar. The uses to which this kind of cloth have been put are easy to comprehend - costume, matting, house decoration, containers. The designs are vibrant and immediately attractive, yet redolent of the individuals and far-flung communities which produced them.

The form of this catalogue follows in general the layout of the exhibition which it has been produced to accompany. The introductory sections describe the various uses to which bark has been put in different parts of the world. Inevitably there is a concentration of examples to illustrate these uses which reflects the strengths of the collections in the Exeter museum. The majority is thus of barkcloth from the islands of the Pacific, together with some examples from Africa and central and south America.

This catalogue is not intended to be a comprehensive account of the uses of bark or the myriad forms of barkcloth, but a survey which opens up some examples in a worldwide context. The list of books and articles in the references will give more detail for readers who wish to pursue the subject further. What the writers hope to have engendered is an interest in a material and a form of artistic endeavour which has not been as well-known and appreciated as it deserves. The catalogue and the exhibition are a means of introducing bark and barkcloth to a wider viewing public.

Cllr. Barry McNamara,
Portfolio Holder for Leisure and Environment,
Exeter City Council

Acknowledgements

The production of this catalogue has been a team effort. We wish to acknowledge the contributions of the following people to its development:

To John Allan, Yosi Anaya, Jane Burkinshaw, Peter Gathercole, Veronica Johnston, Steven Hooper and Donna Sharp for their constructive and positive comments on and contributions to the text. To Sue Minter (Curator of Living Collections at the Eden Project), Penny Hammond (Head Gardener at Saltram), Enid and Teddy Goodwin for their assistance with botanical details. To David Garner for his unfailing patience, enthusiasm and acrobatics in creating the photographs of items in the Exeter museum collections, as well as the National Trust for allowing use of its space to photograph the larger items. To Jeanie Kemp and Messrs Rankins Brothers & Sons for sharing their expertise in the proper use of cork. To John Butler of the Burton Art Gallery, Bideford; Carolyn Wingfield and Lynn Morrison of Saffron Walden Museum; Jeremy Knight of Horsham Museum; Giles Guthrie of Maidstone Museum; and Winifred Glover of the Ulster Museum for their assistance in facilitating the loan or transfer of items or images of items in their museum collections. To Professor Lalage Bown, Morwena Stephens and an anonymous lender for their generosity in letting us borrow pieces from their personal collections. To Alison Blaylock, Veronica Johnston, Jenny Balfour-Paul, Tony Kasule, Kay Pole, Milli Stein, Connie Bland of 'Something Different' and Yosi Anaya for their contributions to the collections with information, items and material from the Solomon Islands, Fiji, the Marquesas Islands, Uganda and Mexico respectively. We would also like to pay special tribute to John Allan for his work with the Pacific collections of the Royal Albert Memorial Museum to reveal the significance of the Bond and Vaughan items.

Len Pole & Sherry Doyal

Contents

List of figures

❙❘ What is Bark ?

Bark is the many layered, outer covering or skin of a tree. Trees grow in many environments and the bark adapts to protect the living tree from its environment.

The outer bark, the periderm, has layers comprising the phellum (cork), phellogen (cork cambium or cork producing cells) and the phelloderm **(fig 1)**. Cork cells are usually hollow and insulate the living stem from arboreal sunburn, forest fire or cold. Thick bark protects the stem from external impacts. The cork cell walls contain wax which waterproofs the stem to protect it from rot or drought. The waxes contribute to the grey appearance of some barks. Resin and tannins contained in cork cells protect the tree from fungi, bacteria and insects. Spines and thorny branches protect the tree from grazing animals and man. It is possible to harvest outer bark because it can be removed without killing the tree and will grow again. Under certain carefully controlled circumstances the inner bark can also be removed without killing the tree; this is done in harvesting bark for making barkcloth in Uganda (Roscoe, 1965:405).

The type of periderm has a strong effect on the appearance of a tree. In smooth barks the periderm continues to expand as the tree grows. But the periderm may be discontinuous; as the tree grows, new periderm forms below the old, cutting it off from water so that it dies. Discontinuous periderm comes in different forms:

○ **Ring bark** has periderm in concentric or continuous ring layers.

○ **Scale bark** has overlapping layers.

○ **Paper bark** has periderm with alternate thick and thin layers; the thin layers fail and the bark separates in sheets to reveal thin, smooth new bark below.

○ **Shaggy** or **string bark** is similar to paper bark but shreds into strands.

○ **Persistent bark** cracks and becomes deeply fissured over time rather than shedding from the tree.

Because the periderm is impervious to water and gases, trees need a way to draw oxygen to the living tissue the bark protects. Lenticels are the lens-shaped pores in bark which allow the wood stem to breathe through its skin. The London plane (*Platanus x hispanica*), grows well in an urban environment because it has a bark that is shed so that new lenticels, not blocked by pollution, are exposed. Lenticels are conspicuous and easy to see in cherry, birch and cork barks but can be microscopic. A bottle cork has the lenticels running from side to side otherwise air would enter the bottle and spoil the wine.

Beneath the periderm a woody stem is encircled by a layer of living cells called the vascular cambium. As these cells divide and multiply the stem expands and, like skin, bark stretches, cracks and is shed to fit the new girth (Prance, 1993). In spring in temperate regions and the wet season in the tropics vascular cambium division is most active so this is when it is easiest to remove bark from the tree. The barkcloth-maker in Boso, Ghana demonstrating the methods he uses, explained his difficulty in separating the inner from the outer bark as being due to the work being demonstrated in March in the dry season rather than the more usual wet season, in July or August (Pole, 2001:4).

The vascular cambium cells divide to form an inner layer of xylem or wood and an outer layer of phloem, or soft bast. Soft bast is a system of fibrous tubes. These draw food sugars photosynthesised in the leaves down to the roots to nourish the tree. If this encircling layer is disrupted by a cut all round the trunk or is completely removed the tree dies. It is this bast layer, the inner skin, which is used to make cloth in tropical climates.

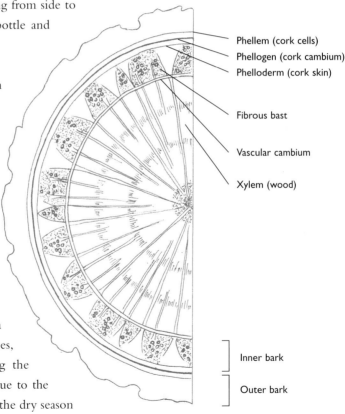

Phellem (cork cells)
Phellogen (cork cambium)
Phelloderm (cork skin)

Fibrous bast

Vascular cambium

Xylem (wood)

Inner bark

Outer bark

Figure 1   Drawing of tree section showing bark layers.

2 | Bark as Raw Material

Medicines and related uses

Figure 2 Samples of bark (*Eucommia ulmoides Oliver*) used as medicine in China for the treatment of arthritis. *RAMM*

Many different world cultures have long understood that phytochemicals (plant chemicals) have medicinal properties **(fig 2)**. University botanic gardens have worked until recently with traditional healers and parataxonomists to try to isolate active ingredients before both traditions and natural habitats are lost (Irwin, 1997:24). Active chemicals are often defence mechanisms to protect plants from predators and damage. They are secondary chemical compounds or metabolites, that is, substances necessary for or formed by the sum total of organised chemical reactions to maintain plant life. Significant groups are: alkaloids (any of a series of nitrogenous organic compounds of plant origin); glycosides (any compound giving sugar and other products on hydrolysis); fungicides and bactericidal resins.

A hundred million people each year are infected by malaria. The alkaloid quinine is extracted from the root and trunk bark of *Cinchona*, a genus of trees of the madder family (*Rubiaceae*) native to the South American Andes. It is still the most effective remedy even though the alkaloid was synthesised in 1944 in the USA. It was incorporated into Indian tonic water to disguise its bitterness and make it acceptable when combined with gin, and is retained in it today as a flavouring. Linnaeus named the plant after the Countess of Chinchon, wife of the Viceroy of Peru, cured of malaria by bark in 1638. It had been introduced by South American First Nation peoples to Jesuit priests in 1633 and via them to the west as Peruvian bark in 1639. Jesuits operated a monopoly from 1651-1660. Alexander von Humboldt and Aimé Bonpland isolated the active alkaloid in 1820 and called it 'quinine' after the Amerindian word *quinaquina* meaning 'bark of barks' **(fig 3)**. Today it is cultivated in Indonesia, Zaire, Tanzania, Kenya, Rwanda, Sri Lanka, Bolivia, Colombia, Costa Rica and India. (Lewington, 1990:163-6).

Cancer drugs are extracted from barks. The South African cape bush willow (*Combretum caffrum*) supplies treatments for colon, ovarian and lung cancers. The phytochemical works by reducing blood flow in tumours, cutting off oxygen and nutrients and therefore reducing tumour growth. Taxanes extracted from the Pacific yew (*Taxus brevifolia*), are used for the treatment of ovarian and breast cancer (Matthews, 2001).

The world's favourite pain-killer is salicylic acid. Better known as aspirin, it can be obtained from poplar and willow bark **(fig 4)**. Salicylic acid is also used as a fungicide and a dye.

Figure 3   Bottle of Indian tonic water containing quinine.

By permission of The Coca-Cola Company

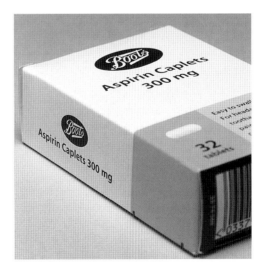

Figure 4   The world's favourite pain-killer, Salicylic acid.

By permission of Boots The Chemist Ltd.

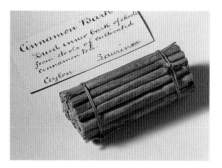

Figure 5   Sample of Cinnamon tubes from Sri Lanka.
RAMM

Figure 6   Advertisement for cork-tipped cigarettes, 1936.
Geographical Magazine

Pau d'arco is a south American tree used in treating a number of yeast-like parasitic fungi, especially *Candida albicans*, a cause of thrush. Its active ingredient is lapachol, derived from its bark (Clark, 2003).

Cinnamon is the inner bark from trees of the Laurel family, particularly *Cinnamomum zeylanicum*, native to southern India and Sri Lanka **(fig 5)**. Traditionally it is used as a medicine, an astringent, an antiseptic and for the relief of flatulence. It has been linked to the relief of type II diabetes (Derbyshire, 2000).

Witch hazel is derived from the bark of *Hamamelis virginiana* which yields an astringent lotion used by native north Americans in treating swellings and tumours. It is more commonly used today as an anti-inflammatory and skin cleanser.

American Buckthorn (*Rhamnus purshiana*), also known as *cascara sagrada* (sacred bark), is used as a laxative and mild emetic. The active ingredient is hydroxymethyl-anthraquinone.

The filtering action of cork was used in cork-tipped cigarettes to absorb nicotine, the habit-forming narcotic **(fig 6)**. Folk medicine recommends the use of cork under a pillow to prevent insomnia or cramp.

Poisons

Curare is a common name given to a range of poisons based on different plants. The most well-known use is as an arrow and spear poison, especially in south America, Africa and south-east Asia. However, it is also used as a muscle relaxant for voluntary muscles in surgery. The active ingredient is the alkaloid cuarine obtained from a number of sources: *Chondrodendron tomentosum* and *Curarea* species of the moon seed family (*Menispermaceae*), also Abuta species.

Curare was unknown in the west until the 16th century, when Spanish conquistadors were in contact with native Amazonians. It remained a secret until Alexander von Humboldt's field account of extraction was published in 1800. In 1814 Charles Waterton developed the under-standing that curare acts on voluntary (eg lung) and not involuntary (eg cardiac) muscles. In 1850 Claud Bernard demonstrated the mechanism by means of the blocking of transmission of nerve impulses to muscles. In 1896 R. Boehem classified three types:

○ bisbenzylisoquinoline alkaloids from the *Menisper-maceae* stored in bamboo tubes (Tube-curare)

○ Strychnos bisindole alkaloids from the Loganiaceae stored in gourds (Calabash curare) (cat no. 1)

○ equal mixtures of these two, stored in ceramic vessels (Pot curare)

The active constituent Tubocurarine was not isolated until 1939. It was introduced into anaesthesiology in 1943.

Closely related to the cuarine alkaloid is the strychnine alkaloid. Sources include *Strychnos toxifera* (vine bark). The bark is scraped, pounded and extracted in cold water. *Strychnos nux-vomica* is an Indian tree; the seeds are a source of strychnine but the bark is traditionally used as a snake bite remedy.

Other plants from the bark of which poisons have been extracted include *Antiaris* species, used in Malaysia for *ipoh* dart poison. *Antiaris* trees are themselves used as sources of barkcloth in west Africa. Woody tropical climbing legumes *Derris* species (active ingredient rotenone) are used traditionally in Malaysia to stupefy fish and now the ground roots of some varieties are widely used in horticulture as an insecticide.

An arrow poison used by Yanomami (of northern Brazil and southern Venezuela), Paumari (Upper Purus river, Brazil) and other tribes comes from the Ucuuba tree (*Virola theiodora*) a member of the nutmeg family (*Myristicaceae*). The active ingredient is 5-methyoxy-N, N-dimethyltryptamine. It is also used as an hallucinogen. The resin is extracted from stripped bark by heating the bark over a fire, collecting it in a receptacle and boiling the resin to drive off the moisture. This concentrate is then pulverised for use as a snuff. The Bora of Peru use a cold-water extraction from shredded inner bark which is then concentrated by boiling to a paste.

An as yet unidentified bark from the Lower Congo was said to have been used as a 'test' in an ordeal in the 1870s (cat no. 2).

Dyes and Tannins

Native Americans use Alder (*Alnus* species), a decoction of bark to darken birch bark for basketry, dye skin, quills, hair and cloth; red, orange, black, or brown tones can be obtained. Salicylic acid from willow (*Salix*), also gives red, black, or grey. Birch bark gives red and brown. Oak (*Quercus*) gives red and grey. Poplar (*Populus*) and plum (*Prunus*) give red, green and purple. These are just a few examples of the use of bark in making dyes – there are others described in Section 4 on barkcloth.

The Maori use tree-bark tannins such as *Manuka* and *Hinau* followed by immersion in iron rich mud. The colour is a complex of ferric iron and phenolic hydroxyl groups of the tannins.

For many centuries, a leather industry has been based around the village of Colyton in Devon. The tanner required good, local water supplies, ox and heifer hides from the local agricultural industry and supplies of bark for tannins. Historically oak bark from Exmoor was used. The bark, stored in a bark barn for three years, was ground and mixed in water to leach out tannins to produce tan liquor (More-Gordon, 2001:132-133).

Russian leather was made by tawing ordinary hides in an oil extracted from birch bark rather than in milk of lime. This process made the leather supple and less subject to rot, mould, and decay. The leather has a characteristic cross hatching, often visible, which is not a decorative feature but is a direct result of the method used to process the leather. The surface of the partially tawed skin was manually broken, perhaps with a sharp edged board, perhaps with a metal or a bone scoring tool, to enable birch oil to penetrate the hide thoroughly. This process was described in 1825 by Beman: 'Calf skins being steeped in a weak bath of carbonate of potass and water, are well cleaned and scraped to have the hair, &c., removed. They are now immersed in another bath, containing dog and pigeon dung in water. Being thus freed from the alkali, they are thrown into a mixture of oatmeal and water to undergo a slight fermentation. To tan these hides, it is necessary to use birch bark instead of oak bark; and during the operation they are to be frequently handled or agitated. When tanned, and perfectly dry, they are made pliable by oil and much friction; they are then to be rubbed over gently with birch tar, which gives them that agreeable odour, peculiar to this kind of leather, and which secures them against the attacks of moths and worms. This odour the leather will preserve for many years; and on account of it, Russian leather is much used in binding handsome and costly books.' (Beman p.108, quoted in Forman, 1988:206-7).

Rotten bark is used to smoke tan skins. Fungi digest out the cellulose leaving phenol-containing lignin behind. The smoke contains phenols, aldehydes and quinines, which both colours and waterproofs the skin (Storch, 1987:1; Rahme and Hartman, 1998:77; Howatt-Krahn, 1987:45).

3 | Bark: fibres, sheet, cork and cloth

Bark fibres used in basketry, textiles and cordage

Bark can be split into pliable, long strips suitable for basketry making. Vine rinds or barks can make very long weaving elements, producing a strong even structure, free of joints. Bark can be also used to decorative effect when colour or gloss is required to contrast with other basketry materials. Japanese basket makers use cherry bark to contrast in colour with bamboo. The colour contrast between the obverse and reverse of birch bark is exploited by weaving with both sides or for containers by scratching through *(sgraffito)*.

The Ainu of northern Japan worked with both elm and lime bark. Attush is the Ainu word both for the elm bast fibre and the textile made from it. It was made into cloth for summer wear (cat nos. 3, 4). There is a loom in the Horniman Museum from northern Japan with warp and weft threads of elm bark set to produce a form of braid. Munro describes the structure and use of the loom used

in weaving bark fibre as well as other vegetable fibres (Ohlsen & Durrans, 1994:21-27). A secondary source of bark was a variety of lime, which produced a coarser cloth not suitable for clothing. Unlike elm bast, it was also used to make cordage.

On the west coast of Canada, among First Nations communities, working with wood is the province of men; the bark is worked by women. Spring and summer months were the best for the removal of bark from the cedar trees, whether red (*Thuja plicata*) or yellow (*Chamaecyparis nootkatensis*). The yellow was thought of as superior to the red because of its greater strength. Stripping the tree always began with a prayer to the tree, asking for its 'dress' to transform into fibre for baskets or clothing for people (Stewart, 1984:113). The uses of the inner bark from the cedar encompassed most parts of daily life. The rough untreated outer bark (cat no. 5) was used for a temporary shelter and it could even be made into a short-term boat for emergencies. However, the bark was mostly prepared by drying in the air and then pounded with a bone mallet (cat no. 6) on a smooth

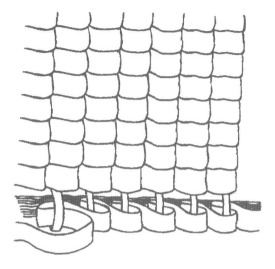

Figure 7   Drawing showing 'imbrication', a decorative
                basketry technique

Jane Burkinshaw

stone, until it became supple and fine enough to be used for weaving. The bark was split into strips and woven into ceremonial head-dresses (cat nos. 7, 8), capes, blankets, rain ponchos, waistcoats, bags, baskets, covers for bowls, mats, and also to decorate masks. The cape (cat no. 9) was made on a frame of uprights with a rope stretched between them, the twining work proceeding from the top down (Burkinshaw, 1999:44). The bark was shredded to make bandages, wash cloths and diapers for babies, and to use as tinder, paint brushes and napkins. It could be dyed red with the bark of Red Alder, for ceremonial head and neck rings (Turner, 1998:66, 67). Baskets were constructed in coils (cat nos. 10, 11) or plain weave, often with wrapped decorative elements. Imbrication is a technique that creates overlapping folds of bark

resembling roof tiles **(fig 7)**. This technique was employed to decorate coiled spruce root basket surfaces with patterns in cherry bark (cat nos. 12, 13).

In the same region the Interior Salish groups pulled off the stringy bark of Big Sagebrush (*Artemisia tridentata*) stems and roots to use for weaving mats, bags, baskets, capes, ponchos, blankets, skirts, aprons, dresses, loin cloths, even socks and shoes. The Okanagan stuffed pillows with sagebrush bark and used it for tinder. Twisted into a rope, ignited and left to smoulder, it was easily transported and used to kindle fires (Turner, 1998:144, 145).

In England willow (*Salix*) is the common basketry material. Contemporary basket makers use brown willow, that is with the bark retained, but the range of bark colours is wide and can be incorporated in baskets to decorative effect. Brown willow is harder to work with than stripped willow as it is less obedient to the worker and care must be taken not to damage the bark in working. Traditional English baskets are of stripped willow, either buff or white. Buff is produced by boiling with the bark intact, releasing tannins which stain the stems light brown, then removing the bark. White is stripped without boiling. 'Green' willow refers to freshly cut stems.

An isolated example of the use of bark fibres in head-wear is the hat from Antigua in the RAMM collection, made from thin strips of tamarind bark and woven with other vegetable fibres into a wide-brimmed hat based on a European model (cat no. 14).

The use of bast fibres in African weaving is patchy but widespread. It is referred to in passing in most surveys of weaving and textiles on the continent. It is mentioned in connection with the non-cotton textile fragments excavated at Igbo-Ukwu, dating from the 10th century, although it is not clear whether tree bast fibres or those from jute or flax were involved. Weaving with bast fibres from Hibiscus species has survived into the 20th century in some areas of southern Nigeria, for specifically ritual purposes associated with death and burial among Igbirra and other Yoruba-speaking areas (Picton & Mack, 1979:31-32; Picton, 1980:75). Bark fibres are also woven into mats known as *gudza* in the Masvingo province of south-east Zimbabwe (Ellert, 1984:90-92). Ellert gives no detail about how the mats are made; in fact, they are twined, sometimes with additional knots for texture and with stripes and patterns of different colours (Johnston, 2003 pers. comm.). Ellert does refer to a Portuguese account from the 16th century, writing of the Batonga of the Mtoko area in the north-east weaving inner bark to make blankets for bedding. A major centre for the use of tree bast fibres in weaving was Madagascar although it survives here and elsewhere mostly as a source of rope. This appears to be the main use for bast fibres in Zimbabwe, according to Ellert, who gives a confused account of the processing of bark into fibre in the south-east of the country (Ellert, 1984:90).

The use of prepared bark fibres in cordage is very widespread. Cedar has been used in twined cordage on the Northwest Coast of north America. Fibres from prepared tree bark and vines have been manufactured by peoples of the Amazon basin (cat no. 15) for many hundreds of years in making straps for back baskets and material for containers such as dart quivers as well as bindings on arrows, bows and blowpipes (cat nos. 16-19); examples from the Xingu national park in the south-east Amazon were collected by Monica Lima Carvalho in 1999 and 2003 for the Exeter Museum (cat nos. 20, 21). Bark fibres were used in making cordage in the Gwembe valley of southern Zambia, near the border with Zimbabwe (Reynolds, 1968:174-7).

Sheet bark used in containers, boats and as a medium for paintings

The use of sheet bark as a raw material was commonplace in aboriginal Australia. Examples include bark shelters, particularly in the more temperate regions (Anon, 1925:106), belts worn in the north-west, headdresses, caps, personal ornaments associated with mourning, coffins, and containers. Paper bark was used as wrapping for pigment and for spearhead tool kits (cat no. 22). Baskets made of bark occur from the Tiwi of Melville and Bathurst Islands, in the Northern Territory; decorated with ochre designs, they are used in mortuary ceremonies to hold gifts. They were often destroyed at the end of the ceremonies (Cooper, 1981:178-179, nos. N303-7). Other examples of bark containers in Australia include a bucket used for carrying water, from Gippsland, Victoria, a folded container with a loop handle from South Australia, and a bowl from the

Northern Territory (Edge-Partington, 1890-98: series II & III). Food-carrying containers of a sheet of bark crimped at the ends are recorded in Western Australia; larger examples were used for carrying babies.

Canoes in the woodlands area of eastern north America were an essential means of transport, since there were over half a million lakes and innumerable rivers (Gidmark, 1988:7). Canoes made of bark have been in use for over 3,000 years (ibid:9) and were still being made in small numbers during the last decade by a few skilled specialists from the Algonquin, Huron, Ojibway (Chippewa), and other native peoples in the eastern states of Canada. The bark was obtained by these groups from the white or paper birch (*Betula papyrifera*) also known as the canoe birch. The outer bark was used; lengths up to six metres could be obtained from a large straight branchless tree. The best time to peel the bark was in August when there was sufficient warmth in the air to make the bark supple. The frame of the canoe was made of white cedar. The bark was carefully scored and cut to shape on the frame. A single sheet of bark was used for the whole length of the canoe, but sections to increase the beam were usually needed. Although the major construction was the work of men, women undertook the sewing of the bark to gunwales using spruce root. The ribs of the canoe frame were inserted and the cedar sheathing was added after the bark had been attached to the frame (cat no. 23). Birchbark canoes were usually used in inland waters throughout the year and could last for many years if well cared for. Accurate models have also made over the past 150 years

by the canoe-makers themselves as well as others (cat no. 24). Paper birchbark was also used to wrap food for storage, to line graves and cover corpses, to splint broken limbs, bind implements and as roofing and siding for temporary shelters. The thinnest birchbark was used for wrapping items, the thickest for canoes. Intermediate grades were used for peaked or domed winter wigwams and for the conical summer lodge, and are still made into a wide range of containers in Europe **(figs 8, 9)** as well as north America (cat nos. 25, 26). For example, the Tahltan made snow goggles from bark, the Dena'ina of Alaska made birchbark hats and also used the bark to make a dye for skins (Turner, 1998:154-156). Birchbark was also used in producing souvenirs for the tourist trade from the early 19th century onwards (cat nos. 27-29).

Spruce bark was widespread and widely used in Nunavut (formerly the Northwest Territories of Canada). The Dogrib, Mountain and Slavey Nations used spruce bark canoes. Temporary spruce bark canoes were made to traverse lakes and rivers – small and light so easily carried into the mountains. They were easier to make than birchbark canoes, although they could only be made in the spring when the sap is rising and the bark can be easily peeled from tree. However, items made of birchbark are more durable. The Iroquois of the eastern woodlands area used elm bark for canoes.

Bark boats were used widely in Australia: from Cape York, a canoe from Johnston River region, (Edge-Partington, series III:95), to sewn bark canoes used in both river and sea voyages in the Gulf of Carpentaria, to the inland waters of the Murray-Darling basin on the Victoria/South Australia border. On the coast of New South Wales and Victoria, craft were made from large cylindrical panels of bark closed off at each end, held open amidships with wood struts and ribs (Anon, 1989:24).

Canoes somewhat similar to those used in Australia have also been described from the Ainu of northern Japan but Munro infers that they were made in a hurry as a temporary substitute when other materials were not available 'probably substitutes for the skin-covered boat' (Ohlsen & Durrans, 1994:33, pls.41-42).

Northwest Coast First Nations use bark of both red and yellow cedar in sheet form in a great variety of ways. Removed from the tree in long sheets and without further modification, it was used for both roofing and flooring for houses. The Cowichan used sheets of bark to make disposable cooking vessels for boiling fish and the Quileute of Washington State made berry storage boxes of folded and stitched cedar bark. In some areas people used larger pieces of inner bark to make canoe bailers, spoons and storage bags (Turner, 1998:76).

Evidence from 18th-century sources suggests that bark shelters in Australia were decorated inside with ochre paintings of hunting scenes. Examples of these have been recorded in recent years such as a photo of a bark hut in Central Arnhemland, Northern Territory, showing paintings on the bark walls (Cooper, 1981:55).

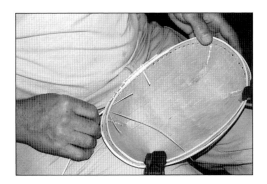

Figure 8   Andre Chapuis making a sewn birchbark bowl in the north American style at the Basketmakers' Association Summer School in 2002.

Veronica Johnston

Figure 9   Jo Merriman, a student at the Basketmakers' Association Summer School in 2002, making a base of plaited birchbark strips for a bowl. The tutor was Ann-Maria Vaatainen from Finland.

Veronica Johnston

Over the last century, the use of bark as a medium for painting has been concentrated on Arnhemland. The early examples from the beginning of the 20th century were painted for use in ceremonies on a number of different media, after which they were allowed to decay. Even in more recent times some paintings were created specifically for sacred purposes, although the great majority are now made for sale.

In Arnhemland, the bark was prepared from the inner section of the stringy bark tree, placed over heat to soften it and allow the flattening to become permanent by weighting with stones. The painting surface is roughened with sand and prepared for painting with a ground colour of ochre, after which the main designs are blocked out in yellow or black. The common colours for the detailed designs are yellow and red from mineral sources, white from clay and black from charcoal or manganese. Morphy provides a description of the painting process in Yolngu in northeast Arnhemland (Cooper, 1981:56-57). There are many hundreds of styles of aboriginal art in Northern Australia alone. The paintings are rarely exclusive to media such as bark, but will also be found on rock, sand, skin, basketry, cardboard and synthetic surfaces (cat no. 30).

The decorative appeal of bark textures and colours as a surface coating or veneer has been attractive to craftsmen worldwide, especially cabinet- and furniture-makers (cat nos. 31, 32).

Cork

The cork oak (*Quercus suber*) grows in several countries in the Mediterranean region – Portugal produces 50% of the world's commercial cork. No cork can be removed for the first 25 years of the tree's growth. The outer bark which supplies cork can be removed without damage to the tree. Once removed, it is left in the forest for seasoning before being transported to the factory, where it is boiled in water for 90 minutes to remove impurities and increase pliability. The planks of cork are then stacked for two to three weeks to flatten and reach optimum humidity for further processing. The planks are graded into seven categories based on thickness, porosity and appearance. Planks which do not pass the grade are granulated for use in other products such as floor tiles.

Only the highest grade planks are used for producing cork stoppers. The chosen planks are boiled again and sliced into strips slightly wider than the final length of the stopper. The strips are punched along the grain of the bark, at an angle to the lenticels (cat no. 33). Machines can punch 45,000 corks a day; skilled workers can punch up to 20,000 of the best quality corks a day. Any waste material is granulated or used as fuel. The corks are finally polished and sterilised. Good quality corks are an essential part of ensuring that wine resides happily in its bottle until required.

Bark cloth

The word 'barkcloth' is not well-known to many people in the UK. Although everyone knows in general about bark and cloth, the production of cloth from bark has never been part of the cultural repertoire of communities in this country. The reason is not hard to find. The kinds of trees which produce bark that can be made into cloth grow plentifully in the humid tropical areas of the world, but not in the temperate regions such as Europe. The annual winter period results in a layer of bark being laid down which is too thick or otherwise inappropriate for manipulating into cloth.

The definition of 'cloth' includes any fabric woven, felted or otherwise formed of filaments. Bark is the skin of a tree or other woody plant. The useful part of the bark from the barkcloth-makers' viewpoint is the inner bark, the soft fibrous tissue inside the more inflexible, corky covering. The combination is a felted mass of fibres. Although it is produced using a number of distinctive techniques, none of them involves machinery; barkcloth production therefore is not restricted by the size or energy requirements of any piece of equipment. A piece of barkcloth can be of any size; many pieces made in the Pacific island group of Tonga were hundreds of metres long. The smallest complete piece in the collection is a table mat 10 centimeters in diameter.

4 | Barkcloth: manufacture and significance

Introduction

The distribution of barkcloth broadly follows the tropical regions of the globe **(fig 10)**. The main centres are in the tropical Pacific Islands, island south-east Asia (the Philippine Islands, Sulawesi, Borneo), east, central and west Africa, central and tropical south America. Although the word 'tapa' is often used synonymously with barkcloth, this is a Polynesian word of Tongan or Samoan origin for the undecorated edge of the cloth. Since in this catalogue a wide variety of cloth is described from all over the world, it will be called 'barkcloth' in general or by the local name when specific pieces are described.

Manufacture

Barkcloth is made from the inner bark or bast of a restricted number of trees **(figs 12-22)**. The tree most often associated with the manufacture of cloth is the paper mulberry (*Broussonetia papyrifera*) a native of southern China, introduced at an early period to island south-east Asia and Melanesia and by means of the ocean voyages of the ancestors of the Polynesians to the Pacific Islands **(fig 11)**. Other sources include the banyan (*Ficus bengalensis*, or Indian fig), used mainly in the Pacific islands and in south and south-east Asia, and the breadfruit tree (*Artocarpus altilis*), found throughout the Pacific, but its use as a source of barkcloth is much more restricted. The common tree for barkcloth in eastern Africa is another fig species, the Natal fig (*Ficus natalensis*). A range of *Ficus* species is used sporadically in central and southern America, including *F. padiofolia* and *F. petiolaris*. Another source of bark for barkcloth-making is the *Antiaris* genus, most usually *A. toxicaria*, a native of the high forest zones of west, east and central Africa. It is the source of cloth in the Ivory Coast, Ghana, and

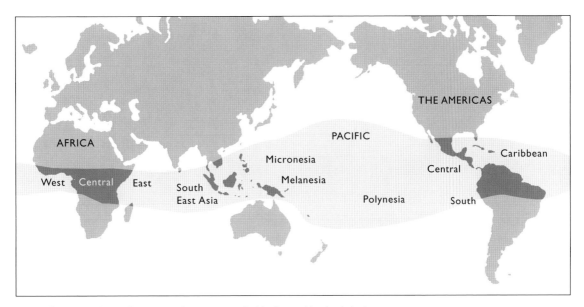

Figure 10 Map of the world showing areas where trees suitable for making barkcloth grow.
RAMM.

Figure 11 Paper mulberry (*Broussonetia papyrifera*) growing in Fatu Hiva, Marquesas islands, February 2001.

Jenny Balfour-Paul

Figure 12 Barkcloth-making in Vatulele Island, Fiji in April 1993: stripping bark from one-year-old stem of a paper mulberry tree. *Veronica Johnston*

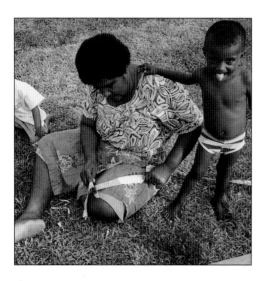

Figure 13 Barkcloth-making in Vatulele Island, Fiji in April1993: Amelia Kaiwalu separating the inner from the outer bark. *Veronica Johnston*

Figure 14 Barkcloth-making in Vatulele Island, Fiji in April1993: Amelia beating the inner bark.

Veronica Johnston

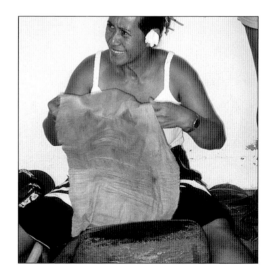

Figure 17 Beating the inner bark of the breadfruit tree, Omoa, Fatu Hiva, Marquesas Islands, on 14th February 2001.

Jenny Balfour-Paul

Figure 18 Holding up the beaten cloth, Omoa, Fatu Hiva, Marquesas Islands, on 14th February 2001.

Jenny Balfour-Paul

Figure 15 Barkcloth-making in Vatulele Island, Fiji in April 1993: Amelia holding up a single beaten strip.

Veronica Johnston

Figure 16 Barkcloth-making in Vatulele Island, Fiji in April 1993: Amelia folding the single strip before beating it again.

Veronica Johnston

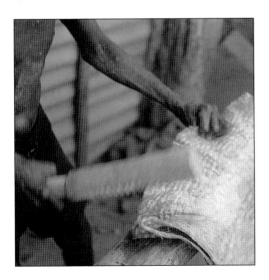

Figure 19 Kwadwo Gyem beating the inner bark of an *Antiaris* species at Boso, Eastern Region, Ghana, April 1973. *Len Pole*

Figure 20 Kwadwo Gyem staking the beaten and washed cloth out to dry, Boso, Eastern Region, Ghana, April 1973. *Len Pole*

Figure 21 Barkcloth maker demonstrating the use of the beater, Kampala, Uganda, March 2003. *Milli Stein*

Figure 22 Barkcloth maker showing the size of the finished cloth, Kampala, Uganda, March 2003. *Kay Pole*

Nigeria. It is also used in the Philippines and the island of Borneo. Its bark is used in rope-making in India.

Antiaris together with the *Ficus* species and the other trees mentioned above are all members of the *Moraceae*, the mulberry family. They grow in tropical forest areas only and are restricted in their distribution, being sensitive to altitude and soil condition. Edel reports of the Kyiga of south-western Uganda, that despite its prevalence in the neighbouring Buganda kingdom, barkcloth cannot be manufactured in their region because, although they live within 120 kilometres of the Equator, it is too mountainous for the right trees to grow (Edel, 1957:81). Barkcloth cannot be made on coral atolls in the Pacific because soil conditions do not allow the growth of the appropriate trees.

The bark is obtained either by cutting the tree down and then stripping a band of bark off the tree (cat nos. 34, 35), or stripping an incomplete band from the living tree, being careful to bind the wound immediately. One consequence of this latter technique, apart from the continued viability of the tree itself, is that the quality of the bark for cloth making improves. This has been reported especially for the method used by Baganda makers, in Uganda. In general, the cloth is produced by beating the fibres of the inner bark, usually once they have been soaked in water or a mud solution. The fibres are beaten on a log using mallets of wood, stone, bone, shell or ivory (cat nos. 36, 46, 52, 61, 62). As a result of this process the layers of fibres felt together (cat nos. 37, 38); the walls of the tissues are broken down, allowing

Figure 23 Decorating barkcloth in Vatulele Island, Fiji, April 1993: Amelia Kaiwalu using a stencil made from an X-ray plate to add a double row of lines to the design. Note other used stencils in the background. *Veronica Johnston*

Figure 25 Decorating barkcloth in Vatulele Island, Fiji, April 1993: Amelia Kaiwalu puts the finishing touches to the central design of rosettes. *Veronica Johnston*

Figure 24 Decorating barkcloth in Vatulele Island, Fiji, April 1993: Amelia Kaiwalu using another stencil to add a brown motif to the design.

Veronica Johnston

the fluid to coalesce with fibres. Layers of beaten fibres can be further felted together to form thicker and larger sheets, or size can be increased by pasting sheets overlapping edge to edge. The dried cloth provides a surface which is in varying degrees capable of taking pigmented decoration **(figs 23, 24, 25)**, utilising brushes, stamps, stencils and patterns transferred from design boards (cat nos. 39, 63, 107).

The cloth, once dried and sometimes dressed or decorated, is used as clothing, bedding, matting, room decoration, shroud, raw material for masks and other ceremonial body covering, and more recently and more mundanely as tablecloth, doyley, wall hanging or other forms of cultural souvenir.

Significance

The view has often been expressed that barkcloth is either a remnant technology surviving only in places where it has not been superseded by something more advanced, usually woven textile of some kind, or an interstitial procedure surviving in culturally retrospective contexts such as funerals, for example in Baganda and Maya traditions. Sayce's account of barkcloth among the Maori is notable in this respect not so much for its description of the decay of the technology, understandable principally due to the sub-tropical climate in which the proto-Maori voyagers found themselves, but because he describes them as having been 'content with clothing of *tapa*' in their former home islands, as if they were dimly aware that something more fitting was just over the horizon (Sayce, 1933:62). However, the point is made by Te Rangi Hiroa, also quoted by Sayce (1933:186) that the use of tapa may have repressed the development of woven textiles, or that weaving was abandoned by the Polynesians and Micronesians.

Sieber suggests the disappearance of barkcloth in Africa was related to its fragility especially when wet (Sieber, 1972:155). However, Turnbull offers the view in relation to 'the forest people' of the Congo jungle that pygmies use of barkcloth as clothing in a humid tropical environment was due to its ease of manufacture and zero cost, but also to the fact that they 'prefer it' (Turnbull, 1961:120). In some parts of the Pacific, incoming Europeans (mostly missionaries) were often hostile to the use of barkcloth. This was due partly to its

importance in relation to traditional religious practices, connected with the spirit world of the ancestors. They also saw it as a 'primitive' technology, to be replaced with imported textiles, the trade in which was under their control. Essentially the issue was about economics as much as technology.

Although there is no doubt that in some areas of the tropical world barkcloth has been progressively replaced as the cloth of choice by woven textiles, there is precious little evidence to show this process in action. It is necessary to go beyond the level of subsuming existence of barkcloth as a footnote in the ethnography of woven textiles, for instance "... in Melanesia the place of textiles is taken by barkcloth" (Cranstone, 1961:55).

Consider examples of the two forms existing side-by-side: in Santa Cruz and in Borneo. In the latter, there was evidence to suggest a connection between the use of barkcloth as costume and head-hunting (Leonard & Terrell, 1980:74), since both were associated with the forest. This could, however, be hearsay transformed into fact by the assumption that they were both thought of as 'primitive' activities; the idea needs to be examined more closely. Woven cloth, by contrast, is a material which has been more overtly transformed by technological intervention. In the case of the island of Ndende in the Santa Cruz group, barkcloth, with its distinctive geometric designs also found on painted wood dance clubs and arrow fore-shafts (Starzecka & Cranstone, 1974:44), is worn as a loincloth or headdress. The woven panels, unique in Melanesia and Polynesia, are made into bags for betel-chewing equipment, mats (also used as stores of wealth), but also used as clothing. Here there would appear to be a notional equivalence in the use of the two kinds of cloth, perhaps to be better understood if the report that the woven cloth was made of tree bast is accurate – other writers indicate its manufacture from unspun banana fibre (Neich & Pendergrast, 1997:125). The painted designs also exhibit similarities in their geometrical basis - elongated triangles and sets of parallel lines set at acute angles occur in both forms. A rare photograph in which both barkcloth and woven cloth appear together on the same person, shows the former as a headdress, the latter as an apron (Neich & Pendergrast, 1997:125), and other men in the picture are wearing barkcloth aprons. The equivalence in the one example could hardly be more clearly demonstrated, which is more than can be indicated for the dichotomy in the other.

There is therefore room for dual interpretations of the relationship between textile and barkcloth; it is too simplistic to simply regard barkcloth as a pre-textile form of cloth. It has distinct characteristics, not the least of which is the ability to be felted or adhered together to form a potentially limitless expanse and to take painted designs and appliquéd motifs without stitching. However, its major advantage as a material is possibly a symbolic one. Barkcloth is utilised as a covering for the human body, alive or dead, as are textiles; or a medium for designs, as are textiles. What is more distinctive is its use, particularly in Polynesia, as a protection for sacred objects and as a prophylactic against their power for the

human beings who come into contact with them (Thomas, 1995:143). The reason barkcloth is able to protect in this way could derive from its transformation from tree covering. There is a relational correspondence between the intermediate nature of the bast layer within the tree and buffering role barkcloth it often assumes in Polynesia and Africa.

It is used as a shroud material in central Polynesia and Uganda. More significantly, it uniquely performed as a substitute human covering in the Marquesas Islands. This was taken to its logical conclusion in the use of barkcloth as an equivalent of human skin. The soft tissue of deceased chiefs was allowed to decompose, the skin being replaced by a wrapping of barkcloth. The skull was kept separately and covered with barkcloth moulded to represent the face, decorated with substitute eye designs as well as figures of sharks. Such chiefly relics were kept in a shrine house, and brought out for important public activities (Kooijman, 1972:194-5). The small barkcloth covered figures from Easter Island were probably used in a similar way. A more recent development of this symbolic association is the employment of tattoo designs on Marquesan barkcloth taken from the principal classic western publication on Marquesan material culture published in the 1920s and since widely distributed in the islands (Thomas, 1995:146,147). This is an excellent example of the vocabulary of tourism being utilised to re-express a vital element of Marquesan heritage.

5 | Barcloth in the Pacific

Barkcloth was known from every island group in Polynesia and Melanesia, although its manufacture was confined to the high islands of volcanic origin. There are few references to barkcloth from Micronesia, due to lack of the appropriate trees on the predominantly low lying coral reefs. The origins of the process are little understood but its widespread occurrence throughout these Pacific island groups suggests that the technique spread at the same time as the ancestors of these peoples themselves from their earliest known homelands in south China and south-east Asia. This is supported by evidence from decoration on pottery produced by the Lapita people between 3,500-3,000 before the present-day (BP), to which barkcloth designs have been convincingly linked (Green, 1979:13-31; D'Alleva, 1998:13). There is archaeological evidence to indicate that barkcloth-making was being practised in southern China and mainland south-east Asia over 5,000 years ago. The main original sources of trees which supply bark suitable for making cloth and paper are in eastern Asia. Cuttings of the trees were carefully transported, together with many other plants, by the voyaging ancestors of the peoples of the Pacific to their new homelands.

Polynesia

The initial populating of the Polynesian islands took hundreds of years, from the first arrival in Fijian islands about 3,500 years ago to the most recent in Aotearoa about 1,000 years ago, also including Rapanui (Easter Island) and the Hawaiian Islands from about 1,200 BP, the Society Islands, including Tahiti, about 1,400 BP **(see fig 26)**. In an examination of barkcloth making and decorating it is useful to distinguish two main subdivisions of Polynesia: central and northern Polynesia, including the island groups of the Society, Cook, Austral, Marquesas, and Hawaii, together with Rapanui to the east, on the one hand; and western Polynesia, comprising the island groups of Fiji, Tonga and Samoa, with their outliers Niue, Uvea and Futuna on the other. Other island groups such as Tuamotu are entirely made up of coral atolls. Aotearoa is outside the tropics, so that, apart from archaeological evidence of barkcloth making, there are no extant pieces of barkcloth from anywhere except the extreme north of North Island.

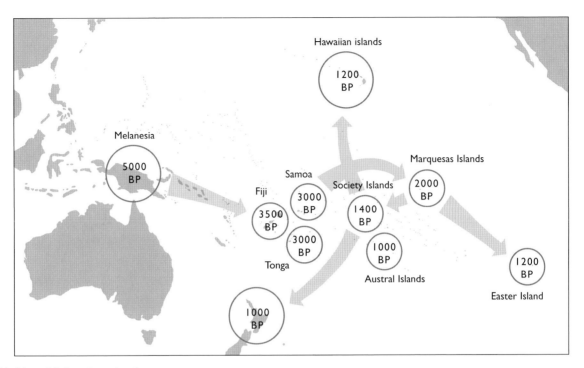

Figure 26 Map of Polynesian migrations. *RAMM*

'Tapa' is the most common name now used in relation to Polynesian barkcloth (indeed it is something of a global referent) but was originally used in a very restricted sense in Samoa and Tonga to refer to the uncoloured edge of the barkcloth as it was being decorated. In Tahiti the cloth is *'ahu*, in the Marquesas *hiapo*, in Hawaii *kapa*, in Tonga *ngatu*, in Fiji *masi*, in Samoa *siapo*.

In central Polynesia the highest status cloth in the early contact period was white and undecorated. Also at this time and throughout the period when barkcloth was the preferred clothing material, almost all everyday clothes were undecorated, but not necessarily white. Up to about 1830 high status European visitors were likely to be presented with high status cloth. On the other hand European visitors at all times were drawn to collect, if not be presented with, decorated cloth. The number of decorated pieces in early European collections does not therefore accurately reflect the quantities of different kinds of cloth produced. The book of samples published by Alexander Shaw in 1787 (cat no. 40) is composed of pieces from the Cook voyage period (1769-1780) and gives the most accurate indication of the variation in pattern and hue in barkcloth from Tahiti, Hawaii and Tonga.

Figure 27 Print of Omai 'a Native of Ulaietea', 1774 by
F. Bartolozzi, based on a drawing probably by
Nathaniel Dance. The original drawing was possibly
commissioned by Joseph Banks. Note the circle
design on the under-garment, which is very similar
to one of the samples in the book put together by
Alexander Shaw (cat. no. 40). *Bridgeman Art Library*

Tahiti / Society Islands

Tahitian barkcloth was made from three types of tree: fig
(*Ficus prolixa* – *aoa* or *are*), breadfruit (*Artocarpus incisa* – *uru*),
or best of all paper mulberry (*aute*). Highest ranking
cloth ('*ahu*) either came in fine white, made from the
paper mulberry, or in natural hues, or red or yellow or
black (cat nos. 41, 42). There are samples in the Shaw
volume of each of these. The designs on the cloth
acquired by F. G. Bond in 1791-2, show remains of
appliquéd designs in these colours (cat no. 43). The red
came from a form of fig fruit or cordia leaves, yellow
from the root bark of the *Morinda citrifolia*. Descriptions
of manufacture and decoration in the literature indicate
that the highest quality cloth was made from the bark of
paper mulberry and was white (Kooijman, 1972:10-15;
Neich and Pendergrast, 1997:85). That made from
breadfruit bark was yellower and coarser. The production
capacity was prodigious; in Tahiti it was reported that
groups of up to two or three hundred women would be
working at once (Kooijman, 1988:23).

The use of barkcloth bridged all social classes in Tahiti,
which made its usage and profusion a good indicator of
social status. Men wore a T-shaped breechclout (*maro*)
(cat no. 44); women wore a larger piece of cloth around
the loins (*pareu*). At work in the fields or at home this
was usually all that was worn. The nobility wore and
displayed '*ahu* in many forms and on all occasions. The
poncho (*tiputa*), a sleeveless tunic coming to the knees,
with a head-hole, was a high-status item, either made of
'*ahu* or finely woven hibiscus matting. Several layers

were often worn, with several further layers of cloth in the form of a cloak (*'ahufara*) over the top, plus sash and turban (as in the Reynolds portrait and the Bartolozzi print of Omai, **fig 27**).

The earliest samples of cloth from Tahiti are very restrained in their decoration. The first descriptions, by George Robertson of the *Dolphin* voyage in 1767, contain no evidence about their decoration, except that there were finer and coarser qualities. Cook voyage examples, many of which exist in the form of samples in books such as the Shaw volume, show all-over colour; red and yellow indicating high status. All the illustrations of female dancers, as well as Omai himself, show the majority of cloth from the Cook voyage period to be undecorated and white. Of other pieces itemised in Kaeppler's catalogue, descriptions only refer to white cloth or in the case of three pieces in Sydney, decorated with red circles and half-circles (Kaeppler, 1978b:130). These can be linked to more detailed descriptions and illustrations in the Gottingen catalogue, (Hauser-Schaublin, 1998:282-4), showing dot, circle and cross designs, which can also be seen on the undergarment worn by Omai in the Bartolozzi print **(see fig 27)**. The only example of more complex designs is in Florence "abstract representations of human figures, fish-bone patterns and schematic animals" not connected with any one Cook voyage (Kaeppler, 1978a:116).

It has been suggested that Tahitian designs were influenced by the trade in tapa from Tonga on Cook's voyages, as well as before the period of these early European voyages. However, the Tongan Cook piece illustrated in the Gottingen catalogue (Hauser-Schaublin, 1998:115 and cat. no. 147) bears little resemblance to any Tahitian designs.

Important developments in design can be discerned from the cloths associated with the Bond collection including the scissor-cut appliqué designs on the mourning costume '*heva*' (cat no. 45) and the cape (cat no. 43) in black and red on white. On both surfaces of this cloth there are some fern printed designs, on the front incorporated into the border and on the reverse in one corner **(fig 28)**; these may be the earliest surviving examples of the use of fern designs. Kooijman suggests fern designs were introduced in 1797 (Kooijman,

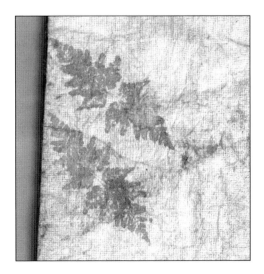

Figure 28 Fern design on reverse of the Tahitian cape collected by Bond (cat no. 43). *RAMM*

1972:21) when the first missionaries arrived, but the Bond piece in this museum was acquired (presumably given to him), sometime between April 1791 and June 1792. More typical fern designs can be seen on the example from the Bandinel collection (cat no. 47), which is unfortunately not accurately datable, but is most likely early-19th century.

Although barkcloth has long since ceased to be manufactured on Tahiti, there were still items of decorative clothing utilising bark elements being made within the last 60 years (cat no. 48).

Pitcairn Island

Traces of habitation were found on Pitcairn Island when the mutineers from the *Bounty* arrived in 1790. These were thought to relate to earlier Polynesian settlers from Rapanui or perhaps Mangareva. The two plain pieces of barkcloth from Pitcairn (cat no. 49) in the museum, acquired by George Peard on the voyage of the *Blossom*, in late 1825 or early 1826, are linked to Tahiti in appearance. These are clearly the products of the mutineers' Tahitian partners, as, most likely, is the beater of whalebone in the British Museum. This is an inappropriately high status material to make a barkcloth beater from, possibly indicating the use of what was available rather than what was traditional; also that it was manufactured by the mutineers themselves. The decorated piece illustrated in Leonard & Terrell from the Field Museum shows appliqué patches with pinked edges in the Tahitian manner (Leonard & Terrell, 1980:23).

Cook Islands

The Cook Islands comprise a northern group consisting of coral atolls, including Manihiki and Tongareva, and a southern group of high volcanic islands. The major sources of barkcloth were Rarotonga, Mangaia and Aitutaki. At the time of the first European contact (1770s -1820s), barkcloth was used as clothing, usually undecorated; a loincloth (*maro*), wraparound skirt (*pareu*), capes and ponchos (*tiputa*), probably though not exclusively, introduced from the Society Islands. The example in the Exeter museum is mid-19th century in date (cat no. 50).

However, the most ritually significant use of barkcloth was in connection with staff gods, which were wrapped in rectangular pieces of cloth with particular sets of design characteristics. These staffs were anything from 80 cm to five metres in length, the cloths themselves up to 60 metres in length. The designs included darkly lined diaper patterns in bands (See Neich & Pendergrast, 1997:77), hand-painted lines of zig-zags, diamonds and sets of lines resembling brick work (see Meyer, 1995:522-3) The most important piece of cloth in the Exeter Museum collection (cat no. 51) from one of Cook's voyages is possibly an example of this form. See Section 8 and the catalogue entry for more detail on this piece.

A completely distinct tradition which developed in the later 19th century was the use of cloth in masks in Mangaia. This may have been built on the pre-existent use of masks associated with religious pageants, intermixed with post-European contact influence from the masking traditions of Melanesia (Neich & Pendergrast 1997:77-79).

Austral Islands

Information about barkcloth from this island group is most fragmentary. Kooijman indicates that first hand information could not be found, other than reports by old women who recreated what they had been involved in as young girls. Sightings of barkcloth clothing were described on Cook's first voyage. The one well-known museum specimen, in the Peabody Museum Salem, shows concentric rings of triangles reminiscent of the discs seen in several kinds of wood carving (Kooijman, 1972:77-79); they may link to sun motifs on house posts and the ceremonial paddles, also feather rosettes worn as head ornaments.

Mangareva, Tuamotu Islands

Most of the islands of the Tuamotu group are atolls and therefore did not produce barkcloth. The main exception is the island of Mangareva, where paper mulberry and breadfruit were used to make cloth called *kau* of finer and coarser quality, respectively (see Hiroa, 1944:431, also Kooijman, 1972:84).

Marquesas Islands

According to Linton, Marquesan barkcloth (*hiapo*) was made from paper mulberry, breadfruit and banyan, a fig species (Linton, 1923:413-414). The collection made by Balfour-Paul includes pieces made from each of these three species (cat nos. 53-60). There are also various references in Melville's novel *Typee*, both to the manufacture

Figure 29　Young Marquesan in February 2001 with a shoulder tattoo representing the eyes of a tiki figure. He is wearing a necklace of wild boar's teeth.

Jenny Balfour-Paul

and uses of the cloth. While it is true that Melville visited Nukuhiva for a few months in 1842, he was not constrained to stick to ethnographic realities in his fiction. Nevertheless, his description of barkcloth making (Melville, 1974:155-6) includes reference to the stripped bast being soaked in running water for two to three days, being beaten repeatedly with mallets carved on their flat surfaces with grooves of varying dimensions, and being 'spread out on the grass to bleach and dry'. All-over dyeing to a rich brown or a bright yellow is also mentioned. This is sufficiently detailed not to be written off as totally inaccurate, but could have been gleaned from descriptions of the Tahitian method. Melville also refers to Tom, his hero, wearing 'a skirt of yellow tappa, like a lady's petticoat' (ibid:127).

Forster, on Cook's second voyage, mentions all women wearing mulberry barkcloth of different sorts, but the variety of cloth was nothing compared to that of Tahiti '... instead of being wrapped up in that number of

Figure 30 Small figure from Rapanui, made of vegetable fibre with sewn cover of barkcloth, and ears of red woollen cloth. The gender is indeterminate, but the figure is wearing a loincloth of barkcloth.

Reproduced by kind permission of the Board of Trustees of the

National Museums and Galleries of Northern Ireland.

pieces, so common among the luxurious chiefs of that island, [ie Tahiti] they only wear a single *ahow* or cloak, which covered them from the shoulders to the knees'. Brigham suggests Marquesans preferred to decorate their bodies rather than the more perishable cloth. He refers to the small number of Marquesan cloths in his collection as '... all well made [but] none are figured' (Brigham, 1911:30). Thomas suggests that the modern designs done on Fatu Hiva are deliberate copies of Marquesan tattoo illustrations taken from von den Steinen's book published in 1925-28 (Thomas, 1995:146-7). This is certainly borne out in the examples collected for this museum by Jenny Balfour-Paul in 2001 **(fig 29)** (cat nos. 54, 55).

Rapanui (Easter Island)

Many aspects of the material culture of Rapanui resemble those of the Marquesas Islands, from which the Rapanuians are said to have voyaged about 1,600 years ago. Phelps refers to the growing of paper mulberry in stone enclosures (Phelps, 1976:86). However, Suggs describes the digging of pits lined with stones to catch rain and retain the moisture of the soil in order to grow bananas and '*ti*' for the manufacture of barkcloth (Suggs, 1960:178). This is a cordyline plant, according to Phelps (1976:86), therefore not so much used for barkcloth-making, but in barkcloth decoration, since it was used as the source of a black pigment by burning the leaves.

At present there is no example of barkcloth from Easter Island in the Exeter museum. This is not surprising as examples are rare in most museum collections. Such samples as do exist are usually seen as part of figure coverings, although an exception to this is provided by the unique quilted piece in the Pitt Rivers Museum (Gathercole, N. D., no. 128). A crouching figure made of a vegetable fibre core with a covering of tapa cloth is in the Belfast Museum (Glover, 1994:44) **(fig 30)**. A janus-faced ceremonial hat with a cane and wood framework covered in painted *tapa* is in the New Brunswick museum (Meyer, 1995:588). The barkcloth covered figure in the Ulster museum is decorated in tattoo designs which are reminiscent of those from Marquesas, as also are the two figures from the Peabody Museum at Harvard, (Gathercole, Kaeppler & Newton, 1979: 136, 137; Kaeppler, 2003: frontispiece).

Hawaii

As in other Polynesian islands, paper mulberry was the most usual source of bark for making *kapa*, although breadfruit and wild fig were also used. Straight trunks of young trees were cut down. The inner bark was softened by wetting, then beaten with wooden mallets until the width of the bark strip was more than doubled (cat nos. 61, 62). Strips were glued together with breadfruit juice or arrowroot and laminated at right angles to make large sheets of cloth. Designs in a variety of colours (black, red, yellow) are either drawn on in freehand or using a long comb or printed using bamboo printing blocks (cat no. 63). Kapa was used for underclothes as in other Polynesian island groups, also shoulder capes (*kihei*) for men and women and multi-layered sleeping mats (*kapa moe*), with a decorated top layer. Distinctive elements in Hawaiian kapa manufacture include extremely fine quality cloth resembling lace in texture, in which the pattern in the beater is clearly visible. Neich and Pendergrast suggest this was a 19th century development, before the importation of woven textiles entirely put paid to *kapa* by the end of the 19th century (Neich & Pendergrast, 1997:92).

The earliest examples of Hawaiian *kapa* come from Cook's first contact in 1778, and are often in the form of small samples made up into the books by Shaw (cat no. 40). A great variety of forms and pattern styles is exhibited in Hawaiian *kapa* (for example, cat no. 64). A small number of pieces have been in the museum for many years; although they cannot be linked to a collector, they have been apocryphally associated with Cook's third voyage. Their condition and colour range leads to the conclusion that this association had no basis in fact (cat nos. 65-71). It is more likely that they were acquired by the museum from the Devon & Exeter Institution at the same time as the Tahitian pieces from Bond, with which another piece has been confused (cat no. 72). Moreover, Kaeppler suggests that these kinds of design distributions are 19th century (Kaeppler 1975). The other swatch is quite recent, demonstrating the revival of interest in the craft as well as the persistence of this form of keeping barkcloth design samples (cat no. 73). It was not until the late-20th century that the craft was revived, using the surviving early sample books and tutelage from barkcloth makers from western Polynesia (see Neich & Pendergrast, 1997:92).

Aotearoa (New Zealand)

Aotearoa is the only Polynesian island group outside the tropics. Because of this barkcloth is not now part of the Maori material culture (although modern interpretations of barkcloth designs on other materials are), since the raw materials did not thrive there (except possibly in the far north of North Island). Starzecka suggests that the paper mulberry would have been one of the plants the first Polynesian settlers of Aotearoa about 1,000 years ago brought with them (Starzecka, 1996:10), and there is archaeological and ethnographic evidence of bark-cloth beaters (Neich & Pendergrast, 1997:88-89). Cook voyagers were shown a small plantation of *aute* trees (paper mulberry) in the Bay of Islands area during their first visit in 1769. By that time and up to about 1840, white barkcloth was made, mostly used for men's ear plugs, although earlier such material had been used to wrap god images, clothing and as covering for kites. The beaters found in archaeological contexts in the north of North Island all show clear connections with the central Polynesian barkcloth-making complex.

There are no examples of Maori barkcloth in museum collections outside Aotearoa, but one piece probably from Samoa was accessioned into Exeter Museum as coming from New Zealand, and could have been obtained there. Maori were initially keen to trade for Tahitian cloth with members of Cook's first voyage, until they realised it was the same material as they were making themselves in smaller quantities. Likewise, 19th century contacts resulted in samples of cloth from other parts of tropical Polynesia being acquired by New Zealanders, either Maori or Pakeha. The later attribution of such pieces to a New Zealand origin by European collectors in these circumstances is not surprising.

Tonga

In both the island groups of Tonga and Samoa, barkcloth was and is usually made using the inner bark of the paper mulberry tree. The tree does not grow to a large girth; sections of the bark produce cloth about 50 cm wide and 1.5 metres long. Large pieces are created in Samoa and Tonga as in Fiji by pasting sheets together at their edges, using arrowroot tuber paste, unlike the felting process used in central Polynesia.

Most *ngatu* is produced in Tongatapu, the largest island, of volcanic origin. The soils in the coral islands are not suitable to grow the paper mulberry tree, which at present is the only source of barkcloth in Tonga, although formerly breadfruit tree bark was also used.

Large sheets of *ngatu* are made up of the smaller sections (called *feta'aki*) beaten out from the inner paper mulberry bark by placing two layers at right angles to each other on a wooden table on which the required designs in the form of *kupesi*, rubbing boards, are set. First the lower layer is put on the boards, having been covered in pigment and glue made from arrowroot. The upper layer is put crosswise over the top, stretched and rubbed with pads dipped in more of the brown pigment. The designs on the *kupesi* gradually appear on the top surface.

How much of the designs appear and how dark they are depends on the thoroughness of the rubbing (see cat nos. 74, 75). In general the designs appear as darker brown motifs on a lighter brown ground. Sometimes the designs are left like this without further emphasis; this is especially true of the earlier *ngatu*. The more specialized task of adding freehand drawn lines as borders or to highlight certain design motifs is left to skilled women (cat nos. 74, 76).

An undyed border is left at each side, which is often used to indicate how many sections have been completed. The length of the cloth made by this method is often over 100 metres; it has been said that pieces over a mile in length were produced on some special occasions in the past. It is this un-dyed area which is called *tapa*, the name for barkcloth which has not yet been given any designs.

There are two major categories of barkcloth in Tonga, *ngatu tahina*, or white barkcloth, meaning barkcloth with a white border, and *ngatu'uli* or black barkcloth. This kind is now extremely rare in collections, the usual pieces being of the 'white variety' for more everyday use such as clothing, bed coverings, room decoration (cat no. 75), and ceremonial presentations. The patterns derive from a wide range of forms: birds, flowers, geometrical shapes or simply the union flag or other crest (cat nos. 77, 78). The black barkcloth was exclusively used for wedding and funeral ceremonies, and consists of black lines on a dark ground and is rarely made today.

More of the *tahina* barkcloth has in the past been made and is still being made in Tonga than in any other part of Polynesia, with an increased emphasis on its significance within a ceremonial context as well as an item of trade. This may sometimes include incidental use as a backing for souvenir items.

Samoa

Decorated barkcloth in Samoa is known as *siapo*. It is made exclusively from paper mulberry bark (*u'a*, which is the name for the tree, the unprepared bark as it is stripped from the tree, and the bast fibres before they are beaten). *Siapo* is decorated in two ways. *Siapo mamanu* is the name for Samoan barkcloth decorated with freehand designs, usually in more than one colour (cat no. 80). The use of design boards, called *upeti*, over which the cloth is placed and rubbed with dye to transfer the patterns to the cloth, results in *siapo tasina* (cat no. 81).

Since the 1920s, these design boards have been carved from planks of wood, bearing designs on both sides. In earlier times and up to the 1930s, boards made from pandanus leaves with lines made from coconut midrib, strips of bamboo and coconut fibre cord were used, tied to a board. In the 19th century, large sheets with many repeat patterns were made using a reddish brown dye. Little freehand overpainting was carried out on these sheets.

More recently, smaller sized barkcloth sheets were produced, often using the wood boards, which were then over-painted to emphasize some elements of the board design (cat nos. 82-85). In a single sample, using a single board, quite different over-painted designs resulted from this procedure. These pieces are sometimes called *siapo vala*, of a size which can be worn as a wrap-around skirt, often by traditional male orators.

Dye is obtained from a number of sources. The most common is the bark of the *Bishofia javanica* (*'o'a*). Other sources are the bark of the candlenut tree, *lama* (*Aleurites moluccana*), and mangrove, *togo* (*Rhizophora mucronata*). Ochre from red earth is also used. Black dye was formerly also obtained from candlenut tree bark. Yellow dye comes from turmeric, *ago* (*Curcuma longa*).

The freehand method is now employed straight onto the prepared cloth, without being sketched in advance, but the artist has a good idea of how the finished design will look before she starts (cat nos. 86, 87). The cloth area for decoration is divided into a number of regular spaces, each of which is filled with motifs outlined in black.

Siapo is used for clothing (cat no. 88), bed covers and blankets, room dividers, tablecloths (cat nos. 89, 90), as well as in ceremonial gift presentation. Before the Second World War, Samoan barkcloth was in plentiful supply, but declined in the 1940s. It underwent a revival in the 1970s (Pritchard, 1984: passim).

Uvea (Wallis Island) and Futuna

The language of the people of Uvea is closely related to Tongan; the general name for barkcloth is the same, *ngatu*.

However, the technology of production is more similar to that of Samoa (Kooijman, 1972:250). The majority of the pieces identified as being produced on Uvea exhibit either individual motifs isolated in panels on a natural ground or repeat patterns from the use of rubbing tablets. The two ponchos in the museum's collection from Uvea have designs rubbed from a board, with added freehand drawing. Some of the geometric designs have been filled in with purple and yellow pigment (cat nos. 92, 93). The information that these are from Uvea came with the objects themselves, supplied by the Revd and Mrs Marriott, missionaries with the London Missionary Society on Samoa for over 20 years between 1878 and 1904.

The Island of Futuna is well known for the production of white barkcloth with extremely fine decoration incorporating grids of cross hatched lines for use as waist garments (*salatasi*). Thomas suggests this design resulted from a deliberate copying of Marshall Islands mat design, but 3,000 miles separates the two (Thomas, 1995:144-146).

Niue

Formerly known as Savage Island, so named because of the unprepossessing nature of the terrain as much as the robust attitude of the inhabitants to Cook's seamen, Niue was not revisited by Europeans until the first missionary landed, in the shape of the Revd John Williams, in 1830. Initially the barkcloth said to come from Niue was indistinguishable from that from Samoa, but in the last two decades of the 19th century a distinct style emerged, often expressed as a grid of square panels filled with intricate designs of geometric shapes or leaf forms in black on a clear white ground of several layers felted together into a stiff sheet over two metres square (Neich & Pendergrast, 1997:71). This efflorescence had disappeared by 1901. The piece which is possibly an example of this style was formerly in the Bideford museum (cat no. 94). Other possible examples include a piece acquired by the Marriotts between 1878 and 1904 (cat no. 95), one from the Hooper collection (Phelps, 1976: no. 531) and a piece in the collection of Graham-Stewart (2001:no. 44).

Fiji

Barkcloth (*masi*) in the Fijian Islands is composed, as elsewhere, of beaten layers of inner bark. The bark of the paper mulberry tree (*Broussonetia papyrifera*) is used to the exclusion of any other. The characteristic way of increasing cloth size in western Polynesia, by pasting layers edge to edge to each other, once the basic beating has been completed, is achieved by laying the bark strips over a long wooden plank, often an upturned canoe.

Masi has many forms and design styles. At the period of first European contact, by far the greater amount of *masi* was plain (*masi vulavula*), but the majority of pieces in museum collections is patterned in a number of ways. There are many styles appropriate to different island groups, some influenced by population movements or trade from communities from Tonga and Samoa. *Masi* is normally made and decorated by women, except in the highlands of Viti Levu, the largest island, where the decoration is undertaken by men.

The plain white cloth was sometimes made from single sheets of the bark of immature trees, producing very fine white gauze-like filament. It often incorporates slightly denser triangles made by overlapping two layers where there is a gap in the sheet caused by a twig hole; this imperfection has been transformed into a deliberate design element (cat no. 96). The plain fine cloth is smoked to produce a rich, variegated brown and orange cloth, called *masi kuvui*.

A distinctive form of decoration which does not occur elsewhere in Polynesia uses stencils, traditionally made of banana or pandanus leaf, but more recently from exposed X-ray film or other appropriate material (Kooijman, 1988:40) **(figs 23, 24)**. The most usual colours are black, made from candlenut (*Aleurites moluccana*), and red or dark brown, from a reddish earth (*umea*), together with the root bark from the *gadoa* tree (*Macaranga seemannii*), and soot in varying combinations. It is the dye produced from this tree (*kesa*) which has given the cloth, which uses the mixture applied with the use of stencils, its name, *masi kesa* (Kooijman, 1977:37-42). The design is built up from the border, in which a limited number of motifs is used repeatedly (cat nos. 97-103). In the enclosed panels individual larger stencilled motifs are placed (cat no. 104). Less commonly, isolated small stencilled motifs in black are randomly situated on the white cloth, often without a border of any kind.

Freehand designs are added using a brush made from a section of pandanus fruit, with finer lines added using a section of bamboo. Freehand decoration is used extensively, often in combination with stencilled motifs. The most distinctive style is associated with the Cakaudrove District of south-eastern Vanua Levu and the neighbouring large island of Taveuni. The cloth is crisply and repeatedly folded, the edges so produced being marked with black dye. Once flattened, the outlined panels are infilled with dye, extra leaves being used to mask off the white areas. Edging bands of stencilled decoration are also incorporated into the design. This was a popular form of decoration (cat no. 105). A variant of this style consists of very fine stencilled designs in black in large diamond patterns, associated with Taveuni island (cat no. 106).

Design boards of various styles have also been in use for many years. Those of Tongan origin are called *kupeti*, made of sheets of pandanus leaves onto which patterns are stitched using coconut leaf midribs and coir thread, often with subsidiary lines of string stitching (cat no. 107). These are most commonly found on the Lau islands to the east, and closest to Tonga. The designs produced with the use of *kupeti* sometimes stand alone (cat no. 108) but are also combined with stencilled or Cakaudrove-style freehand designs or outlining in the Tongan style (cat no. 109). Flat wooden boards with motifs carved in relief are of Samoan origin. Another form of decoration used on Viti Levu utilizes a length of large diameter bamboo incised with grooves of different widths (cat no. 110).

Masi has always been an important trade item between Fijian communities, not all of whom made their own, but may have specialized in other goods such as a fine matting or pottery, and also between Fijian islands and Tonga and Samoa. Historically *masi* was only worn by men, women wearing a different form of vegetable fibre clothing called *liku*, but this distinction was broken down under the early influence of European missionaries in the beginning of the 19th century. However, vast amounts of *masi* were produced for ceremonial gift exchange between chiefly families as well as for inter-island trade both within the Fijian islands and throughout western Polynesia. See for example the illustration of "a chief enveloped in loops of bark cloth" (Roth and Hooper, 1990:69). More recently, as with other Pacific island groups, the needs of tourists for this commodity have become pre-eminent, influencing form and designs.

Melanesia

New Guinea

The vast island of New Guinea is the most culturally diverse region in the world. Over 700 separate languages are spoken. It is not surprising in this context that the occurrence of barkcloth in New Guinea is not universal, although where it does occur it is likely to have been part of a material complex stretching back thousands of years. It is therefore also likely that the former existence of barkcloth making in cultural regions now no longer supporting it will be discovered as archaeological work is undertaken in the island. It does occur in the north coastal area of south-east Papua New Guinea, in parts of the Papuan Gulf, in the central mountains, as well as the Lake Sentani area in north-east Irian Jaya. Many kinds of plants have been used as raw material, not just paper mulberry, but also breadfruit, fig and mangrove species. Beaters are made of wood, but also shell or stone. New Guinea barkcloth is usually made in small pieces, mainly for breechclouts, skirts, head coverings and mask-coverings, rather than the large felted lengths found in western Polynesia. Men are more often involved in the processes, particularly in making decorated cloth for ceremonial purposes.

The best known use of barkcloth in New Guinea is in the masks of the Elema groups of Orokolo Bay in the Gulf of Papua. The most common are the *eraho* mask types (cat no. 112). These are quite common and of a huge variety. The rarer form is *hevehe*, much large and flatter, also using cloth stretched over a cane or wood frame.

On the north coast of Papua New Guinea in Collingwood Bay and adjacent bays of Oro province paper mulberry cloth is highly decorated by women in freehand designs in red, black and brown (cat no. 113). Barkcloth has also been reported from the Trobriand Islands and other parts of the Massim district.

In the Anga area of central mountains both men and women wear plain brown barkcloth cloaks, also used as bed covers, made from fig species. In the central New Guinea highlands some Mountain-Ok groups make and wear barkcloth cloaks. Elsewhere in this highly fragmented region bark, bark fibres and cloth are used for a variety of major and minor purposes – bark for belts, variously decorated and worn only by fully initiated males, fibres to make *bilum* or bags, cloth to wrap feather decorations for dances in men's houses, as underpinning for wigs used in big *moka*, for wrapping a newly deceased man's wealth in order to divine the cause of death (O'Hanlon, 1993:26,32,37,70; Craig, 1988:14-17).

In the Lake Sentani area barkcloth is used as a loincloth with fish motifs. This was developed in the 1920s as a commercial venture (Meyer, 1995:73) and is still thriving – their products are now being sold via a website (www.dewakoku.or.jp).

Bismarck Archipelago: Admiralty Islands

Aprons worn by married women on ceremonial occasions are made of soft thick barkcloth decorated with pendants of black seed cases and white shell money beads (Neich & Pendergrast, 1997:136); see also an undocumented piece illustrated in Leonard & Terrell (1980:39).

Bismarck Archipelago: New Ireland

Although rare, examples of decorated barkcloth exhibit designs which also occur on *malagan* carved wood figures from New Ireland (Meyer, 1995:468). It was also used as adjuncts to masks themselves (ibid:344). The top-knot on the mask in the Exeter museum collection, dating from the 1860s, is made of a small section of plain coarse barkcloth (cat no. 114).

Bismarck Archipelago: New Britain

There are several masking traditions in this large island in which barkcloth plays an important part. It is used most famously as a covering to the masks of the Baining of the Gazelle Peninsula in the east of the Island. Breadfruit bast is used, for both masks of night-time initiation ritual events and daytime mourning ceremonies. The Nakanai of the north coast use masks of barkcloth stretched over a wooden framework in funerary rituals; they are usually buried with the body (Neich & Pendergrast, 1997:136-153; Meyer 1995:368-71, 376-79; Newton, 1999:256-7)

Solomon Islands

Barkcloth in the Solomon Islands (which culturally includes the islands of Bougainville and Buka, although politically they are part of Papua New Guinea) is found mainly on the central islands of Santa Isabel and the New Georgia group. The most common trees from which barkcloth is made are species of banyan making a reddish/brown cloth, and a white cloth from another source, as yet unidentified, but probably the breadfruit (Cranstone 1961:56). The white cloth is often dyed blue, using a form of indigo, with motifs of fish, human figures and a distinctive 'key'-like design. These cloths were a speciality of Santa Isabel Island, often traded to other islands as in the example collected by Brenchley in the Maidstone museum (cat no. 115) (Brigham, 1911:62; Meyer, 1995:407). In the far north of the Solomon Islands, on the island of Nissan, but linked culturally to New Ireland, masks and headdresses of bark fibre have been collected (Newton, 1999:278).

Santa Cruz Islands

Breechclouts and cylindrical head-dresses were made of barkcloth, decorated in rectangular panels filled with fine hatched diamond designs, and called *lepau*. The source of the cloth is paper mulberry (Cranstone 1961, p.56). Most evidence points to the island of Ndende as the manufacturing centre. This is the largest island of the group. Production was started again here in the 1970s. The Exeter Museum piece was made in 1998 (cat no. 116). Other designs include motifs similar to that on this piece which are derived from those on dance clubs, boards attached to rings of feather money, and loom woven bags and ceremonial aprons. The threads used in weaving these cloths were themselves made of inner bark fibres.

Vanuatu

The main areas of barkcloth production were in the central islands (Efate and the small islands of Tongoa, Nguna, Emae) where the cloth was usually of a single colour on each side, trimmed with feathers at both ends, and the southern islands of Erromango, Tanna and Eneityum (Bonnemaison, Huffman, et al, 1996:129-140). It was also known in the northern islands as a base for masks and as sleeping mat material. The craft died out on all islands but Tanna by the early 20th century. There is some evidence of barkcloth belts still being made on Tanna until recently, and the procedures were revived for a brief period during the beginning of the Second World War when the supply of European-made clothing dried up and before the arrival of American troops. This revival was sufficient for a new generation of barkcloth makers to learn the craft and in 1984 it was passed on by them to a Vanuatu Cultural Centre field-worker. This new work was continued with the opening of the new cultural centre in 1995 and the unveiling of a newly created piece of cloth by Moses Jobo (Huffman, 1996:47-56, fig 6).

Most Vanuatuan pieces in museums are from Erromango, including the one in the Exeter museum, collected in the early 20th century. They were called *nemasitse* in the language of the island. The sheets were made and decorated by women and used by women as a cape, for ceremonial display and in exchange transactions such as bridewealth payments (cat no. 118). The cloth was made from various *Ficus* species, principally banyan, but also mangrove. Decorative pigments come from the Indian mulberry (*Morinda citrifolia*). Designs were of fish, flying fox, leaves, and simple human figures representing events or ceremonial scenes.

New Caledonia

Very little is known about barkcloth on these islands, merely some illustrated items incorporating barkcloth elements, such as the lizard charm illustrated in Edge-Partington from a sketch made in the Noumea Museum by Charles Hedley, with a body bound in barkcloth (Edge-Partington, 1898: series III). A barkcloth beater is illustrated with the comment 'New Caledonian beaters are works of art in themselves' (Leonard & Terrell, 1980:36-7). Another wood beater from the Loyalty Islands with a round section is in the British Museum (Cranstone, 1961:56). He also indicates that paper mulberry was used for making barkcloth on the Loyalty Islands.

Micronesia

The island groups which make up Micronesia (Caroline Islands, Kiribati, Marshall Islands, Marianas Islands, Nauru) are almost all coral atolls and therefore in general do not support the kind of vegetation which could be used for making barkcloth. Even on the small number of high islands, of volcanic origin, such as Guam in the southern Marianas, and the Palau islands, Yap and Chuuk, in the Carolines where barkcloth producing trees could grow, they were not used for that purpose. Only the people of Pohnpei were said to have produced barkcloth from breadfruit and also, but less importantly, paper mulberry and wild fig. There are one or two other instances, such as the isolated island of Kapingamarangi, south of the Carolines, where barkcloth from breadfruit has been reported. The sole use appears to have been for clothing such as poncho-like garments (Kooijman, 1972:145-156).

South-East Asia,

especially Indonesia and the Philippines

The earliest datable evidence of the manufacture of barkcloth in any of the island groups of the Pacific comes from the region of south-east Asia. Kooijman links technical details of barkcloth manufacture by Toraja groups of the central Sulawesi region in Indonesia (Hitchcock, 1991:37), with Polynesia – the use of similar sized wood anvils having the same name

tutua, fermentation of the bark strips in the initial stages of manufacture, and many similarities in motifs (Kooijman, 1972:422-442). The squares of barkcloth (*fuya*) from this region are mostly used for turbans and are decorated with elaborate and brightly coloured square and circle designs (Meyer, 1995:93).

The occurrence of items, usually clothing, made of barkcloth in Indonesia and the Philippine Islands is sporadic but widespread. In the Mentawei Islands west of Sumatra, loin coverings of barkcloth were replaced by cotton garments within the last century. Incantations used by *datu*, Javanese healers, have been recorded in a specialised script on concertina sheets of barkcloth, called *delawang* (Meyer, 1995:44). Rough loincloths are used by the Semang of the Malay peninsula. Strips of striped barkcloth are used as festive clothing by Batak and other groups of Palawan and Luzon Islands in the Philippines (Leonard & Terrell, 1980:40, 41). Dayak groups in Kalimantan made ceremonial sleeveless jackets (*bajo*) of barkcloth, highly ornamented with reticulated beadwork, cotton and hawk feathers, said to have been used by headhunters (Leonard & Terrell, 1980:74). There is a much plainer jacket in the Exeter museum (cat no. 119); also a similar piece illustrated in Meyer (1995:93).

6 | Barkcloth in Africa

The major barkcloth producing centres of eastern Africa are Uganda, the upper Congo Basin, and to a lesser extent Ruanda, Malawi, Zambia and the southern Sudan. There are several pieces in the Exeter Museum from the Buganda kingdom of Uganda. Barkcloth was also formerly produced in separated parts of west Africa, from Liberia to south-east Nigeria and Cameroon and including Akan-speaking peoples of Ghana and Ivory Coast. Sieber makes the assumption that the intermittent recorded examples of barkcloth occurrence in Africa south of the Sahara over four centuries suggest widespread use. While this might be a reasonable assumption, there is little evidence for its use in many parts of the continent, such as most extensively in the southern region (Sieber, 1972:155).

The main uses of the material have encompassed ordinary clothing (eg for hunting, in Asante and Boso, Ghana), ceremonial clothing (eg of the Asantehene during Odwira ceremonies in Ghana; masquerade costume in Igala, Nigeria; costume for chiefs and their successors in Buganda, and as costume of the ancestors in Kuba kingdoms of the Democratic Republic of Congo), for bedding (Ghana, Uganda), as room decoration (on the floor of the King's palace in Buganda; hung from the ceiling in Asante), as shroud material (in Buganda, Bunyoro), and most recently, as examples of craft items for tourists.

West Africa

Occurrence of barkcloth in Liberia was reported by Towerson as a result of his first voyage to the coast of Guinea in 1555-56. Sieber reports the presence of it in western Ghana in 1958, also in northern Nigeria, as well as its use by the Igala in dance costumes of painted bark cloth (Sieber, 1972:227, fn 71), the same is illustrated in Picton & Mack, (1979:40). They refer to the Asante of Ghana trading barkcloth widely with other forest peoples of the Akan-speaking area between Asante and the Ivory Coast (which suggests that barkcloth-making was itself not commonly made in this area). They emphasise the chronological priority of barkcloth-making in places where it and locally woven textiles co-existed, such as the Bakuba kingdoms (Picton & Mack, 1979:42-3).

Barkcloth was still being produced in small quantities (cat no. 120) in the Guan-speaking area of the Eastern Region of Ghana in 1972, where it was clearly thought of as referencing the past, and for the majority of the population represented an out-moded technology when compared to both traditional narrow-strip cloth manufacture very much in evidence in local markets, and industrially-produced textiles from the coast, less than 100 miles away. The species used to make the cloth in Ghana was *Antiaris*. The tree was cut down, the bark removed and beaten using a circumferentially grooved round section mallet. It was then washed thoroughly, wrung out and pegged on the ground in the sun to dry **(figs 19, 20)**. The most common and most recent use was as bedding since it discouraged ticks and other bugs (Pole, 2001:8).

In the Ivory Coast, in central savannah areas, bark from *Ficus* species was used to make bedclothes up until the 1960s. The Baoule offered the opinion that the well-prepared barkcloth made their skin soft and smooth (Holas, 1949, 1960:27).

Some elements of patterning on woven textiles suggest the possibility of transfer from their former use on barkcloth in west Africa. The form and procedure of the stamped design on cloth made in the Akan-speaking areas of Ghana and known as *adinkra* are curious when thought of as having been developed for woven textiles, but gain more credence when put in the context of use on barkcloth. The use of stamps is not known on woven textiles elsewhere in Africa and the dye exhibits a coarseness appropriate to the texture of barkcloth as it historically occurs in that part of west Africa; moreover, it is known in the context of barkcloth decoration in Uganda. The ink used in the stamping process is itself made from a bark infusion combined with iron slag; the *adinkra* cloths are decorated by pegging the cloth out on the ground, a procedure similar to that used on the Boso barkcloth in drying it. Also *adinkra* cloths are specifically associated with funerals and mourning, as are many examples of the use of barkcloth in Africa. This association of similarities does no more than suggest a linkage which is worthy of further study.

East Africa

The best known and best-recorded barkcloth making centre in Africa was and is that of the Baganda in central Uganda. The most common tree source of the bark is the *Ficus natalensis* known in *Luganda* as *mutuba*, *mutome* or *olwa*. The work was undertaken by men. The best trees are grown in the district of Rakai, about 150 kilometres south-west of Kampala, close to the Tanzanian border. Each house would have had access to its own tree which could yield up to 40 sheets (Roscoe, 1965:405). A strip about an inch wide and 16 inches long is cut, soaked in boiling water overnight and left in the sun to dry. It is then beaten with a wooden mallet until it becomes much wider and three times as long **(figs 21, 22)**. The same washing, drying and beating process is repeated on following days, using mallets with finer grooves. Pieces like this are used as prayer mats and in witchcraft. The final piece can measure as much as 6 feet by 10 feet. Patches may appear which are carefully sewn with raffia thread, using pieces of cloth taken from the edge. According to notes in the National Museum of Uganda, the bark-cloth process developed in the 15th century during the reign of Kabaka Kimera, king of Buganda. Miniature mallets are on display there; these were made to be sent to men unwilling to continue the arduous cloth-making process as a punishment; the person would be set the task of making the cloth using only the miniature mallets, as a cure for his laziness (Kasule, et al, 2003). Some of the cloths in the Exeter Museum have been decorated using wooden stamps dipped in muddy water mixed with the bark from the *kaboga* tree (cat nos. 121, 122).

One of the main uses of barkcloth in Buganda was for shrouds for the recently dead, particularly for members of the nobility, also by the successor to the dead person. Barkcloth is also used as costume, especially by supporters of the Kabaka, in the general context of the use of material associated with Baganda traditions. The form of the costume is a *busuti* for a woman (a tailored two-piece suit of missionary origin) (cat no. 123), and a shirt for a man **(fig 31)**, although traditionally rectangles of cloth were worn toga fashion (cat no. 124) (Nzita & Mbaga, 1993:18). The cloth is also used for room furnishings – curtains, wall-hangings, floor coverings, tablecloths and blankets. Sheets of cloth are used as surfaces to dry coffee beans, seeds, or to cover anthills to catch flying ants (a useful source of protein). Strips of cloth were also used incidentally as trimmings to costume of other materials, usually skin (cat no. 125).

Figure 31 Woman's *Busuti*, and man's shirt, both of barkcloth, worn by the owners of the barkcloth shop in Kampala, Uganda, March 2003. *Milli Stein*

More recently the most common use is in the tourist market place: decorated hats, purses, coasters, mats, coffee-bean bags, etc (cat nos. 126-131).

Central Africa

The Bambuti of the Ituri forest in north-east Congo use several species of vine. The outer bark is removed from the inner and discarded. The inner bark is soaked in water or mud and further softened by smoking it over a fire. The hammers used to beat the bark strips are made of elephant ivory, the tusk secured in a wooden handle. The cloth is prepared by men and decorated by women. Different varieties of vine give a range of qualities of cloth which are enhanced by dyeing and decorating, usually with red from another bark source, black from gardenia fruit and citrus fruit juice for a light blue. The base colour of the cloth may itself be fawn, brown, blue or white. Turnbull describes the women's patterns as '... of straight lines crossing the cloth with unconventional pygmy geometry'. The barkcloth as worn is kept in place by elaborately-braided belts also made of vine. As elsewhere in the world, fashions in barkcloth change, in base colours, in the designs and the way the cloth should be worn (Turnbull, 1961:120, 121). Sieber illustrates an example of barkcloth from the Ituri forest, collected in 1959 (Sieber, 1972:159). Plain pieces of cloth from the eastern Congo and further north-east in the southern Sudan areas reinforce the suspicion of this as an additional centre of barkcloth manufacture (cat nos. 132, 133).

In Angola and southern Congo as well as north-western Zambia, masks of the Chokwe are associated with male initiation ceremonies under the general name of *Mukanda*. Such masks, representing animals, particularly lions, may be made by Chokwe artists for Lunda ceremonials associated with the boys' initiation camp; the tall conical mask played a pivotal role in the mukanda initiation ceremonies centring on circumcision (Hackett, 1996:98-102). Similar functions are suggested for barkcloth masks in the Lisbon museum collection, from the Lunda and Lwena, also Ambwela of the Cuando-Cubanago area, representing ancestors (Anon, 1972, nos. 387, 402).

7 | Barkcloth in the Americas

Introduction

Steward reports that the first evidence for the cloth in north-west Amazon is from the earliest levels of Huaca Prieta in Peru, dating from over 2000BCE (Steward and Faron, 1959:196). In relation to Central America, von Hagen records that the Toltecs had bark-paper books which were first used between 200BCE and 900CE together with evidence of stone bark beaters in the earliest Mayan period (von Hagen, 1957:56, 183).

Central America

The Maya made and used a kind of paper, called *huun*, for over 800 years. It was made from a species of wild fig. The bark was cut two palms wide and about 20 feet long, and beaten with a ribbed mallet, producing a sheet 40 inches wide, more or less the same length and 2 mm thick. The Mayans used it as clothing as well as paper. Priests continued to wear barkcloth costume after cotton cloth became available. Mayan paper was used for building plans, maps and daily records, usually folded screen style. The Codex Dresden is made of *huun*, using the bark of the *Ficus padiofolia*, folded into 39 leaves. The vast majority of codices and other Mayan books were destroyed by Spanish monks such as Diego de Landa, fearing they contained idolatrous material.

Bernal Diaz, writing of the conquest of the Aztecs by forces under Herman Cortez, reports the steward of Moctezuma keeping an account of all revenues due his master in two books made of *amatl*, fig bark paper, and that he had a 'great house' full of such record books (Diaz, 1963:228). According to Vaillant, *tonalamatl* were 'books of fate' or reference books for priestly guidance made of long strips of *amatl* prepared and coated to take paint, then folded screen-wise, each double leaf opening to show instructions to be followed for one week (Vaillant, 1950:190). The coating was probably the same as the process described by von Hagen, being polished using hot smooth stones, producing a paper whiter than European examples of the same period. The tree was called *amaquahuitl* (lit. 'paper tree') (von Hagen, 1957:183).

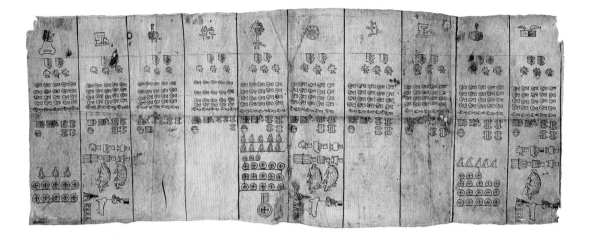

Figure 32 Codex Tepotzotlan, drawn on Amatl paper, c.1555-1556, Tepotzotlan, Mexico, 40 cm by 110 cm.

Reproduced by kind permission of the Board of Trustees of the National Museums and Galleries of Northern Ireland.

Most *amatl* was used as document paper for recording transactions, accounts, land records and maps, records of migrations and trail documents. The Codex Tepotzotlan, in the Ulster Museum, Belfast is an example (Moctezuma, 2003, no. 360). It was created in about 1555 and contains no Spanish paraphrases, even though it records evidence in a case presented to a Spanish judge about tribute demands by Tepotzotlan nobles **(fig 32)**.

Yellow bark paper was sold in large sheets. Bernal Diaz describes sections of the markets set aside for particular goods including *amatl*. There were major production centres such as Amacoztitlan and Itsamatitlan in Morelos State, using the *Ficus petiolaris* tree to make yellow paper in great quantities. *Amatl* was both common and highly valued throughout Aztec society. Although mainly used

as paper for record purposes, other decorative items such as crowns, flowers and streamers were produced; every phase of Aztec life was marked by paper decorations and ornaments (von Hagen, 1957:183-5).

Some of this regard for bark paper persists in the central highlands area of Mexico where the manufacture of *amate* survived the conquest. The reason for its survival was due to the inaccessibility of the villages in the Otomi area and to the ritual importance of *amate* in their complex ceremonial life, in which the local pantheon co-exists with Catholicism. The demand for *amate* paper has increased in recent years. Other Otomi villages of western central Mexico have taken up *amate*-making as part of the local economy. Since the 1960s Nahuas from Guerrero purchased *amate* from the Otomi to use as a medium for highly colourful paintings for general sale both to local people and tourists, borrowing motifs from the regional ceramic ware (Sayer, 1993:83). The older *amates* in the Exeter collection depict such motifs as birds and flowers painted with gouache (cat nos. 134, 135). More recently the painted and drawn designs have evolved and multiplied as more families have taken up this trade. In the last few years trees supplying bark have been over stripped, leading to a shortage. The paper comes in a number of shades, depending on the source of the bark. The wild fig tree (*xalama*) and the mulberry (*moral*) make the whitest paper, other sources include the nettle tree (*jonote*) producing darker shades (Lewington, 1990:198). These are combined to make a paper with characteristic swirling markings, produced as the cooked bark is laid out before being pounded. This is used as the medium on which genre scenes in a bright variety of colours are painted. The new painted *amates* are representations of events in village life (cat no. 136). They incorporate multiple activities occurring at the same time as the main event, which could be a wedding, Christian nativity play, a bullfight, a village celebration with fireworks, or the harvest (Anaya, 2003).

A distinct tradition, using cut out figures in single colours pasted in sets of four onto a paper ground of a contrasting hue, is a product of the Otomi in the Pahuatlan region. The figures are of local gods to which offerings are made (cat no. 137). Bark paper-making also exists on a small scale for ritual use among the Nahua group of the northern Veracruz region in the east of the country (Anaya, 2003).

South America

Masks and body coverings associated with spirits of the forests have traditionally been made using barkcloth as a base material or covering on which designs are painted by peoples of the north-west Amazon. (Anon, 1972, nos. 15, 16, 17; also Steward & Faron, 1959:312). Masks, called *Yakokosutiro* ('clothing of tears') are made by Tukano Indians of the Upper Negro River. A body mask, face and clothing of beaten bark is worn as a single piece. The figure represents a mythical being or animal; the mask is worn by men at funerary ceremonies held one month after burial. The figures are burned after the ceremony. Among other Tukano groups on the Brazil–Peru border similar masks, known as 'tails' come out at every ceremony marking the different stages of individual existence, such as girls' puberty ceremonies (Braun, 1995:44-48, 88), also illustrated in 18th and 19th century engravings (Carmichael, 1985:31). The use of bark in these contexts, together with other forest products is specifically related to the requirement to represent forest spirits in material appropriate to that environment, in contrast to the milieu of the initiate. Barkcloth has also been used for small decorative belts (cat no. 138), but there is no evidence to suggest a similar symbolic referent. Another major use of barkcloth is in the making of simple ponchos in the southern Amazon area of eastern Bolivia (Phelps, 1976: no. 1716) as well as the Jivaro region of Ecuador (Braun, 1995:37).

Caribbean

One of the least known products from Jamaica (and other islands in the West Indies) is a form of bark produced from trees of the genus Lagettaria (Shaw, 1787: no. 39). When the inner bark is retted and beaten it spreads to form a net-like arrangement of fibres usually referred to as lace-bark. No purpose has been recorded for which the Carib, Arawak or other aboriginal inhabitants of the West Indian islands used the cloth, unless it be as a brush (cat no. 139). However, Europeans living there, particularly white women associated with the plantations, experimented with ideas of its decorative use or even as an export item which could earn money for local inhabitants. One example is the child's costume with bonnet which was made in the 1820s at the suggestion of the Lady Cornwallis, given to the Saffron Walden Museum soon after its foundation, in 1833 (cat no. 140). A second example is a book of doyley designs made from elements of lace-bark, again to suggest ways in which the product could be economically useful. The book of samples is undated, but is likely to be early-20th century in date (cat no. 141). The first page of the book contains the following:

'The Doyleys are made from the bark of the Lagetta lintearia tree, growing in Jamaica ... Sold for the benefit of the Orphanage for girls in Kingston, Jamaica'

8 | How did these pieces of cloth get from the Pacific to Exeter?

The acquisition of the pieces described in this catalogue began with the period of European exploration of the Pacific which began in the later 18th century, with the voyages of Cook and others in the 1760s and 1770s, Bligh on his second voyage in 1791-3, Peard on the *Blossom* in 1826, Brenchley and Veitch in the *Curaçoa* (sic) in 1865; also James Agassiz, the collector of the cedar bark cloak, who was on the voyage of the *America* in 1845. Later collections were made by missionaries such as John Marriott in Samoa sometime between 1878-1904. The story is brought up to date with the items collected by Derek Cudmore in the 1970s, also while on diplomatic service in the south Pacific, and most recently of all Jenny and Glencairn Balfour-Paul in the Marquesas Islands in 2001. This latter is an example of a collection being made on behalf of this Museum, taking advantage of their presence in the regions while on a holiday cruise.

The fascination generated by everything associated with the early European voyages into the Pacific islands was nowhere more keenly expressed than in relation to this exotic fabric. One of the earliest references to barkcloth being an article of exchange occurred in 1767, early in the voyage by Wallis of HMS *Dolphin* to Tahiti, two years before Cook's first arrival.

One of the most enigmatic pieces of barkcloth in existence is the piece in the RAMM collection obtained on one of Captain Cook's three voyages to the Pacific islands **(fig 34)** (cat no. 51). The story of its journey from central Polynesia to Devon is little documented and therefore imperfectly understood. It was acquired by the museum in Exeter from the Vaughan family. The entry in the museum's accession register merely refers to '… 9th Nov 1868 E1263 Cloak made of bark of Paper Mulberry? South Sea Islands. Presented by Mr Vaughan. In case G Ethnological, very fine'. It had been acquired by an earlier member of the Vaughan family at the sale of a large number of items acquired by Cook during his three voyages. These pieces had been in the famous museum of Sir Ashton Lever in London, which was put up for sale in 1806. The sale catalogue refers, even more cryptically, to 'no 3147 [A large specimen of] … Otaheite cloth'. The piece is clearly of central

Polynesian origin, but cannot be pinned down more closely (see catalogue entry for details of the various opinions about it). Although there are a small number of pieces with similar designs, the Cook barkcloth example in this collection is the only example of this kind clearly associated with the Cook voyages. A piece of similar design in the British Museum may be a Cook piece, but Kaeppler did not include it in her *Artificial Curiosities* catalogue (Kaeppler, 1978b:160). There are many other examples of barkcloth of this period from central Polynesia, for instance in the collections at Gottingen, Berne and Florence, as well as London, Oxford and Cambridge, all from Tahiti, the great majority of which are plain and white; one of the few patterned pieces, in Florence contains motifs unrelated to the Exeter piece (Kaeppler, 1978a:116).

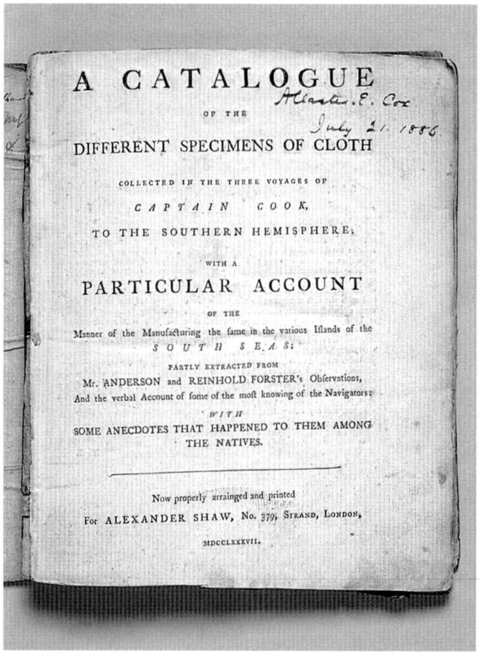
A CATALOGUE
OF THE
DIFFERENT SPECIMENS OF CLOTH
COLLECTED IN THE THREE VOYAGES OF
CAPTAIN COOK,
TO THE SOUTHERN HEMISPHERE;
WITH A
PARTICULAR ACCOUNT
OF THE
Manner of the Manufacturing the ſame in the various Iſlands of the
SOUTH SEAS;
PARTLY EXTRACTED FROM
Mr. ANDERSON and REINHOLD FORSTER's Obſervations,
And the verbal Account of ſome of the moſt knowing of the Navigators:
WITH
SOME ANECDOTES THAT HAPPENED TO THEM AMONG THE NATIVES.

Now properly arrainged and printed
For ALEXANDER SHAW, No. 379, STRAND, LONDON,
MDCCLXXXVII.

Figure 33 Title page of a book of barkcloth samples published by Shaw in 1787. *RAMM*

Many examples of Polynesian barkcloth were first brought to the attention of Europeans in the form of small samples made up into books by Shaw **(fig 33)** and others (Kaeppler, 1975). About 30 of these books were produced, examples of which are in museums in Vienna, Florence, Berne, Chicago (Leonard & Terrell, 1980:11, 29), Sydney, Christchurch, Wellington, Gottingen and the Bishop Museum, Honolulu. Some of these volumes are still in private hands. The interest in these small souvenirs was such that even smaller pieces were cut from some of the volumes and framed. Kaeppler suggests that the majority of the examples she has seen were of Hawaiian origin, which would be expected since the delicate and small-scale nature of many of the Hawaiian designs lend themselves to such treatment (Kaeppler, 1978b:117). If this is the case, the book of samples (cat no. 40), on loan from a local Devon family, is unusual in that the majority are Tahitian (20 out of 39), seven of which are plain white and four patterned. All but one are from the Cook voyages; the exception, from Jamaica, was acquired at the Duchess of Portland's sale. This volume has been in the same family since 1886.

Inevitably there are examples of intriguing and possibly important pieces which have not survived. One such is 'The dress of Omai'. As mentioned above, Omai was the Tahitian who, inadvertently, was brought to England on Furneaux's ship, the *Adventure*, in 1775. He was taken under the wing of Sir Joseph Banks who accompanied Cook on his first voyage. He was the first Tahitian to visit this country and particularly in the fever of exoticism which gripped English society when Cook himself returned, became a required adornment at society gatherings in the later 1770s. His portrait was famously painted by Sir Joshua Reynolds in 1776; a print by Bartolozzi, from another portrait by Dance, became popular **(fig 27)**. In both of these Omai is wearing what appears to be a Tahitian costume made of bark-cloth. A tantalising entry in the Minute Book of the Devon & Exeter Institution (DEI) for April 1823, which records donations to its museum, states: 'The executors of Lady Thomond 'The Dress of Omai, an Otaheitian Prince' '. Lady Thomond had Devon connections and was Reynolds' niece. Moreover she inherited the contents of his house and studio, most of which were sold in 1821. The studio probably contained a number of garments for his sitters, but the Omai costume, if it was among these, was not sold in 1821. Although the DEI transferred the surviving artefacts in its possession to the newly founded Albert Memorial Museum in Exeter between 1868 and 1872, there is no mention of the dress in the museum's register. The BBC film about the Reynolds painting suggests that Omai himself chose the cloth he wore, although it was not made clear what evidence there is for this. In one sense it is likely, since it is copious, in varying degrees of white and undecorated, therefore in Tahitian terms a high status cloth. Indeed it would have been higher status than he would have been allowed to wear in Tahiti or Raiatea, so as an upwardly-mobile Tahitian, exactly how he would wish to be portrayed. As has already been mentioned, a considerable quantity of plain white Tahitian barkcloth had been given to various members of both Cook expeditions, some of which would have been available to Omai, most obviously through Banks. As John Allan remarks in his unpublished manuscript article relating to early Polynesian items in Exeter museum 'The unlabelled, voluminous robes and turban in which Omai posed for the … [Reynolds] … portrait may not have been readily recognisable as being of especial interest' (Allan, 1996). It is also prudent to point out that the light-coloured cloth in this portrait may not have been barkcloth at all. Whatever its material characteristics, it is a sad gap in the present context.

The most important collection to have a connection with both Polynesia and Exeter, and this a more direct one, is the material brought back by Francis Godolphin Bond from his period as First Lieutenant with Bligh's second expedition in Tahiti between April 1791 and June 1792. Allan has fairly conclusively demonstrated that a highly significant addition to the museum's collections in 1868 included a number of these items (Allan, 1995). Although some of them, for example 13 pieces of barkcloth (cat nos. 41-44), were entered in the museum register as having been donated by Bond to the Institution, the most important Tahitian item, a chief mourner's dress (cat no. 45), had no such linking data in the entry. However, in February 1815, the Institution minute book records the donation by Captain Bond of

Figure 34 World Cultures galleries in Royal Albert Memorial Museum, showing catalogue numbers 45 and 51. *RAMM*

a 'Dress of a native of Otaheite'. This in itself was unusual and significant since none of Bond's other donations was listed. Work by both Allan and D'Alleva serve to conclusively link the mourner's dress in the museum's collections with the presence of the then Lt Bond on Bligh's second voyage to the Pacific in 1791-93, especially by reference to another cloth in the British Museum collected on the same voyage by midshipman Matthew Flinders (Allan, 1995; D'Alleva, 1995). Bond retired in 1801, later moved to Exeter and became actively involved in the affairs of the Institution, being a proprietor between 1813 and 1826. The presence of the mourning dress from Tahiti and other highly important pieces of barkcloth in this museum testifies to the significant and continuing role played by Devon people in the developing connections between England and the Pacific in the late-18th century **(fig 34)**.

This theme continues to be demonstrable into the 19th century by means of items from George Peard. Peard was First Lieutenant on HMS *Blossom*, captained by Beechey, which in 1825-1828 explored the northern Pacific and its Arctic waters in preparation for an investigation of the north-west passage. In addition the ship was required to survey the islands between Pitcairn and the Society group (Gough, 1973). Peard spent the last years of his life on the western side of the Exe estuary, in Exminster, where he died in 1831, three years after returning from the Pacific. His collection of items from the voyage was given to the museum in 1916 by his grand-daughter Helen Peard. It consisted mostly of a highly significant collection of Inuit pieces, but also items from the Pacific survey area, including two pieces of plain white barkcloth from Pitcairn. Clearly connected to the Tahitian tradition, these pieces were made some-time between the arrival of the mutineers and their Tahitian companions (seven women and six men-servants) on the island in 1790 and 1827. Realistically the most likely period of manufacture of this cloth would have been soon after their arrival. Illustrations of other Pitcairn barkcloth samples show watermarks and simple dentated bars which Kooijman suggests were 'a local improvisation' (Kooijman, 1972:92) made by the daughters of the women who accompanied the mutineers. The Peard pieces have no such pattern and could be taken for Tahitian cloth (cat no. 49). No details exist of how Peard acquired these two items, although he does mention the making of barkcloth in his Journal.

Chronologically the next important bark item acquired from the Pacific rim region was the cedar bark cloak acquired by Lt James David Agassiz in 1845 from Cape Flattery in Washington State. He was First Lieutenant on the HMS *America* under Captain John Gordon. Agassiz' collection is small but consists of choice items, apart from the cloak, including two very fine wood feasting bowls and a Coast Salish canoe with two paddles. Unlike the other items so far considered, these items were donated to the museum by Agassiz himself in 1869, together with the information in which we can there-fore be clearly confident (Allan 1996). The cloak was made by a woman of the Makah nation from yellow cedar bark and was originally trimmed with sea otter fur (cat no. 9). Such cloaks were used by high ranking people (Burkinshaw 1999:44).

The single item of relevance to this catalogue obtained by the museum from Messrs Veitch & Sons, the well-known firms of nurserymen in Exeter and London, should be understood in two contexts. On the one hand it is part of a much longer story of the gradual and incidental accumulation of items by plant collectors employed by this distinguished business; on the other it is an element in a particular collecting foray on one Pacific voyage. John Gould Veitch was the grandson of the firm's founder and the only member of the family to collect extensively. He first went to Japan and China in 1860 and in 1865 obtained a passage on the voyage of the HMS *Curaçoa*, in the company of Julius Brenchley. The death of his father, in 1847, allowed Brenchley the means to undertake a series of worldwide journeys over a 20 year period. He was in Sydney in 1865 and was offered a place aboard the *Curaçoa* by Commodore Sir William Wiseman. The trip was undertaken in order to investigate reports of ill-treatment of British subjects in south Pacific islands within the British sphere of influence (Waite, 1987:9). Veitch was also allowed to join the voyage, having had permission from the Admiralty to be aboard. The itinerary covered Fiji, Tonga, Samoa, the Solomon Islands, Vanuatu and New Caledonia and the voyage lasted from June to October 1865. Although the principal purpose of Veitch's presence on the ship was to collect plants for his nursery business he also took a keen interest in artefact collecting. In a letter to his aunt on 5th August he says 'My cabin would amuse you. It is hung all over with clubs, spears, fans, mats, etc., etc., curiosities that I have picked up on the islands' (Waite, 1987:91 fn.11). The items collected by Veitch included material from Fiji, Tonga, the Solomon Islands, Santa Cruz and Vanuatu. The only barkcloth piece is probably from the island of Viti Levu in the Fiji group (cat no. 110). There is a similar piece in the Brenchley collection, now in the Maidstone museum (cat no. 111). The two pieces may have been made in the same workshop; in her account of the Brenchley collection, Waite makes the point that 'stops in the various ports were brief', so there was little time for leisurely forays into the surrounding countryside by either collector. In the exhibition, the two pieces are displayed side-by-side, undoubtedly the first time they have been in the same space since a selection of the items collected on the voyage was exhibited in Sydney in November 1865. Veitch came home bearing his precious cargo of plants and also his 'curiosities' (Shepherd, 2003, pp.152-154). Although John Veitch was at that time living and working in London, and his artefacts were initially put on display with others from other Veitch plant collectors in their museum in the Chelsea nursery (see illustration in Shepherd, 2003:118), all the items so collected were eventually given to the museum in Exeter, the family's home town, in 1880, when expansion plans for the Chelsea site caused the closure of the Veitch museum.

A number of items from the collection of the Revd John and Mrs Marriott came to the Exeter museum via their great niece who lived near Kingsbridge, Devon. It had been part of the missionary display in Manchester in 1905, after the death of Revd Marriott at the age of 54 in 1904. John Marriott worked in Samoa between 1878, when he was appointed a tutor in the London Missionary Society Training Institution at Malua, and 1904. Malua is a town on the north coast of Upolu in Western Samoa and was the main centre of the London Missionary Society on the island. In addition to bible studies, Marriott taught horticulture, carpentry and boat building. His collection was built up over the time of his stay in Samoa. Apart from a number of pieces of barkcloth from Uvea (Wallis Island), as well as Samoa (cat nos. 85, 88, 92, 93, 95), it contained mats, baskets and fans, mostly items made by Samoan women. It also included some canoe models which may have been used in the boat-building studies course.

A more recent collector was Derek George Cudmore. He was born in 1923 and served in the Royal Navy from 1942 until 1946 when he joined the Colonial Service as an administrative officer. He undertook tours of duty in Nigeria, Rhodesia, and became Financial Secretary in the Solomon Islands between 1957 and 1967. He was Governor of the British Virgin Islands 1971-74. After he retired he took a job as development officer in Tonga in 1975 for two years and in the New Hebrides (now Vanuatu) in 1980. After his death in 1982 his widow, then living in Honiton, gave a selection of items from the Pacific islands to the museum. It consisted mostly of what a retired colonial officer would have been presented with in the Pacific – shell garlands, necklaces, fans and barkcloth (cat no. 77-79), all well-made and from the 1975 period.

9 | Catalogue

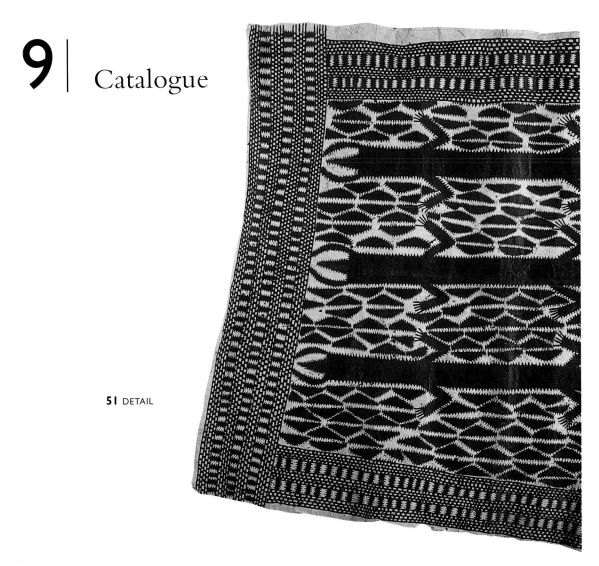

51 DETAIL

All photography by David Garner,
except numbers 52, 62 (Martin Prothero), 107,115 (Maidstone Museum), 140 (Saffron Walden Museum), 141 (Len Pole)

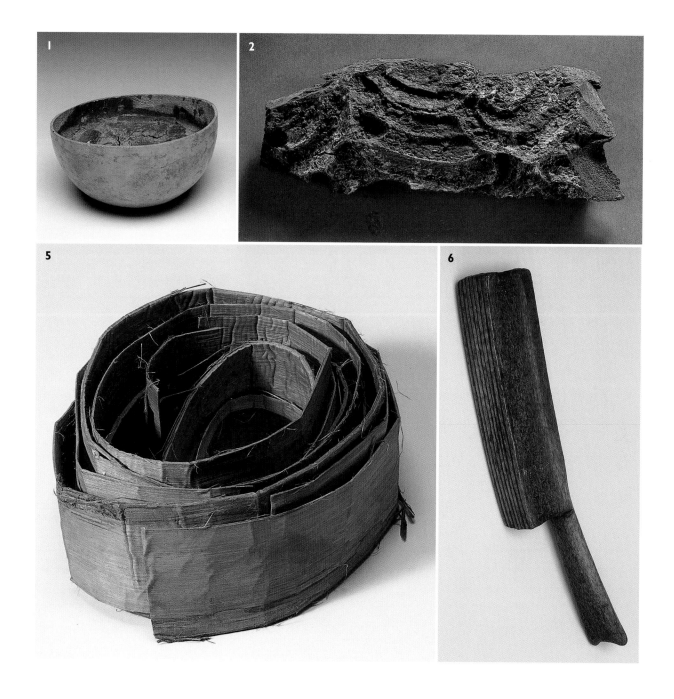

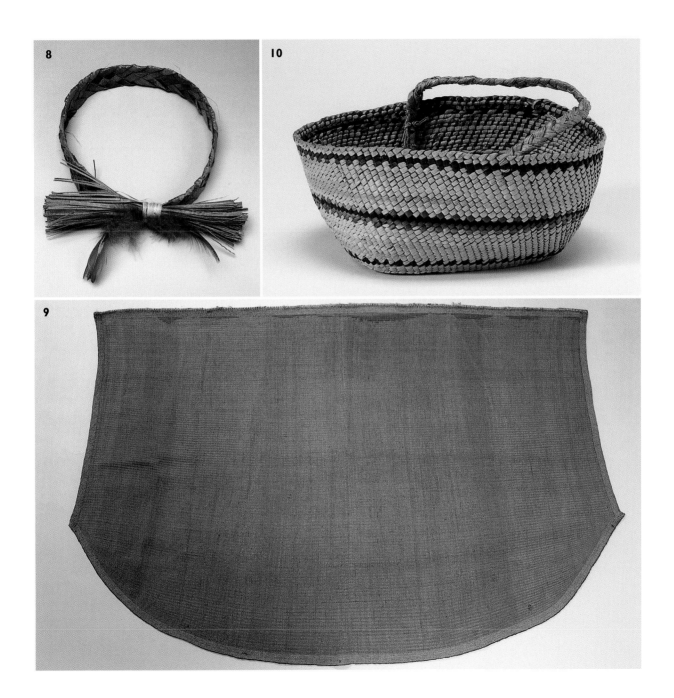

17

18

19

Water Juice (Bamboo)
Botocudo Ind.ⁿˢ
Brazil. Rio Doce.

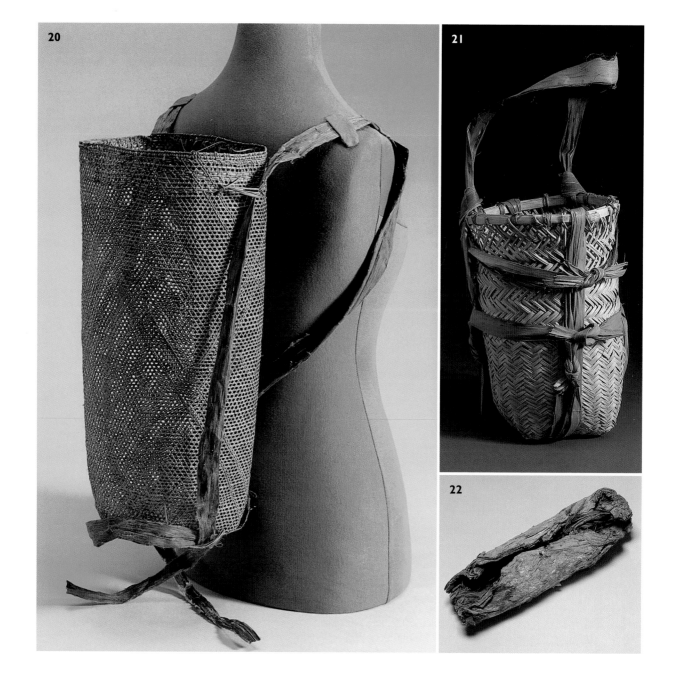

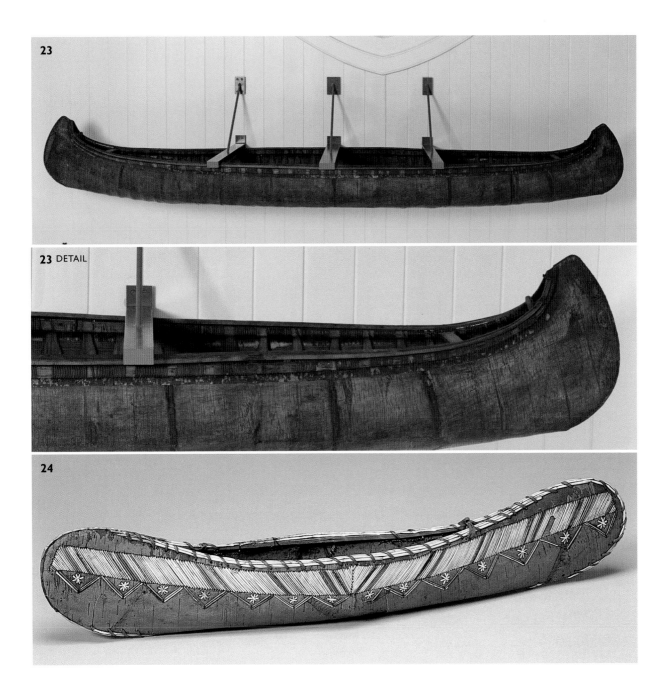

23

23 DETAIL

24

25

26

28

27

30

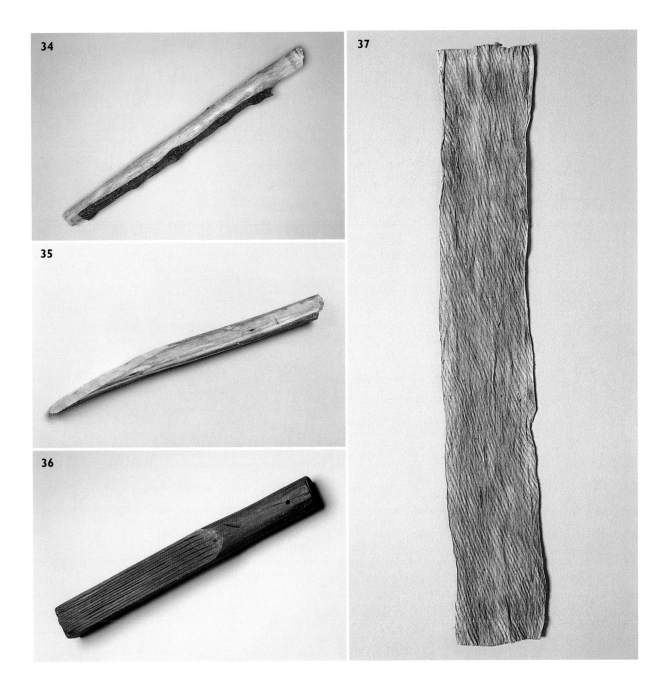

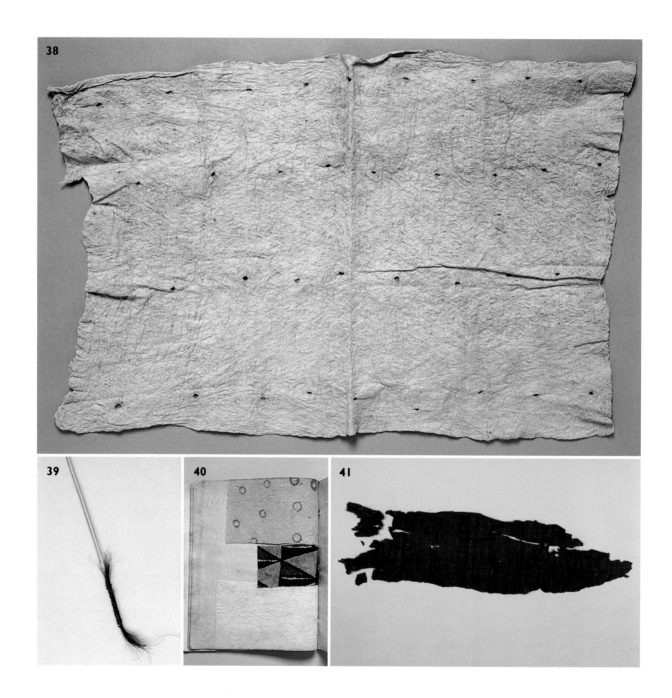

43

44

45 FRONT

45 BACK

46

47

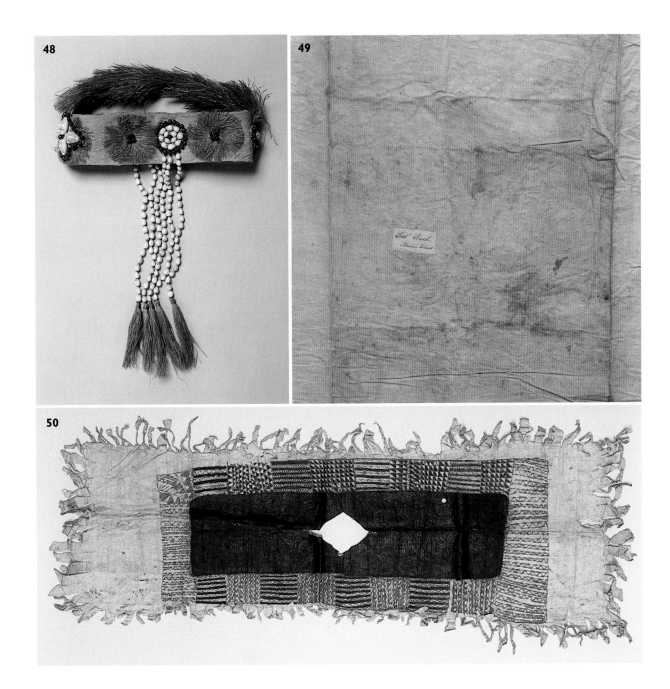

51

52

53

54

55

56

57

58

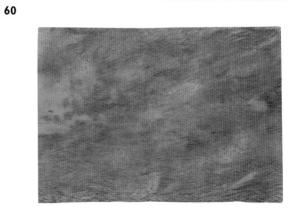

59

60

61 & 62

63

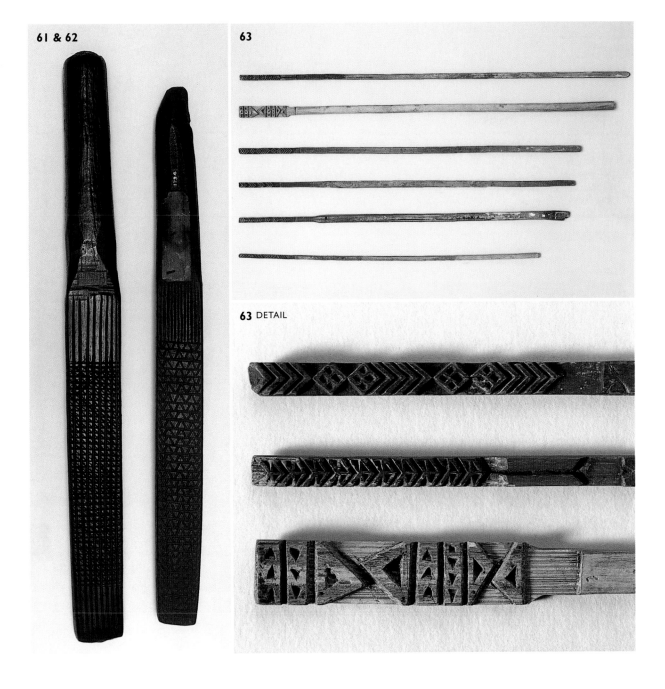

63 DETAIL

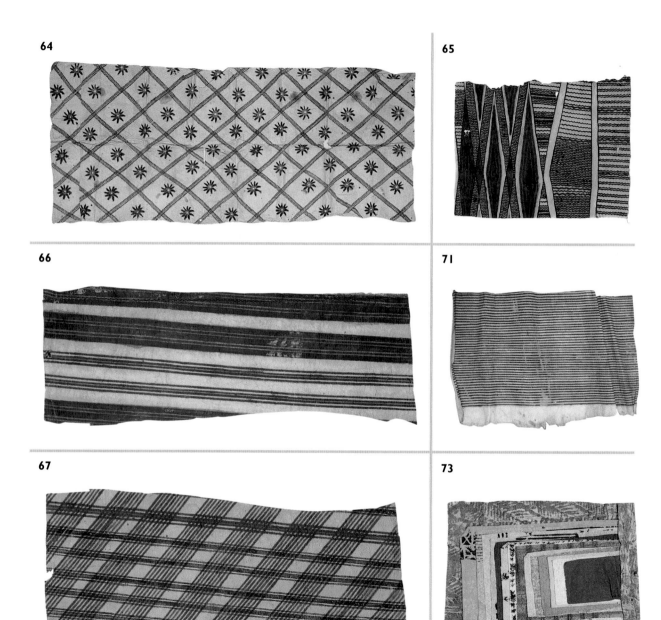

64

65

66

71

67

73

72

74

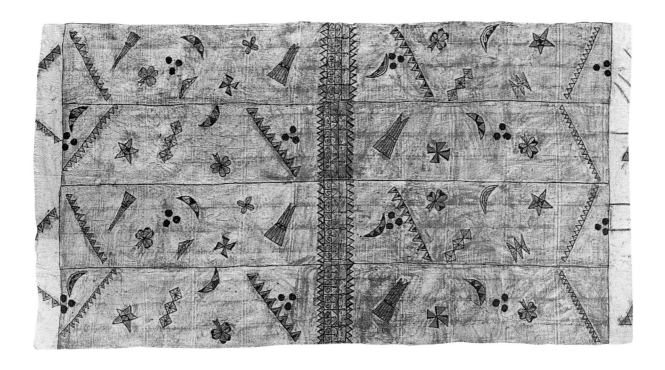

75

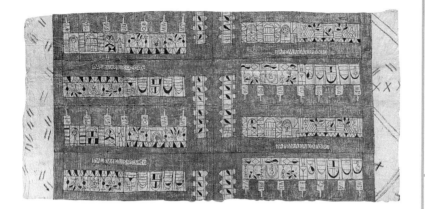

76 DETAIL

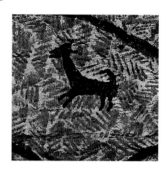

77

78

79

80

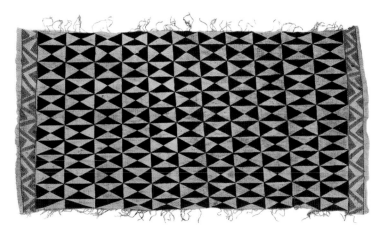

81

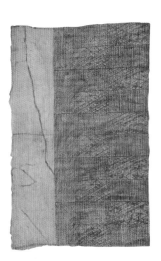

82 (SEE FRONT INSIDE COVER FOR REVERSE)

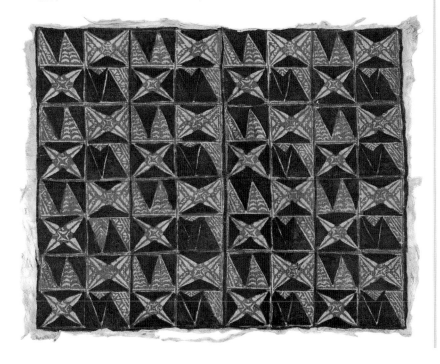

83

85

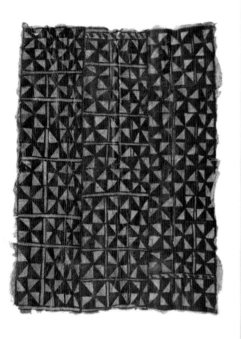

84

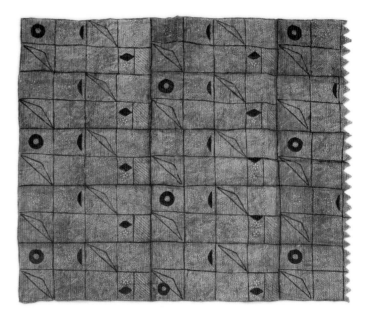

86

87

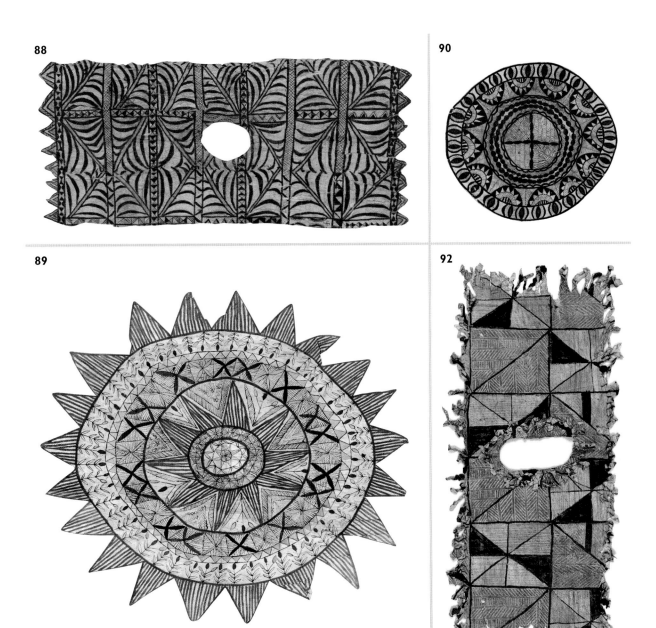

93

95

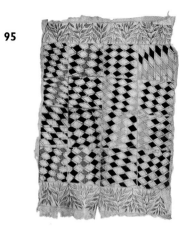

94

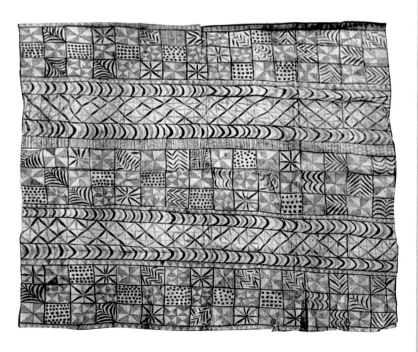

96

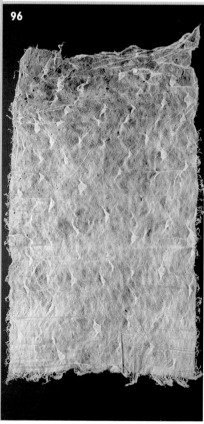

97

98

99

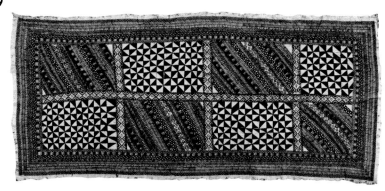

100

101

102

104

105

103
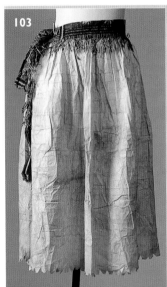

106

107

108

109

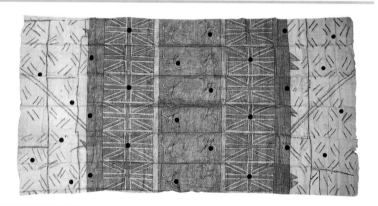

110

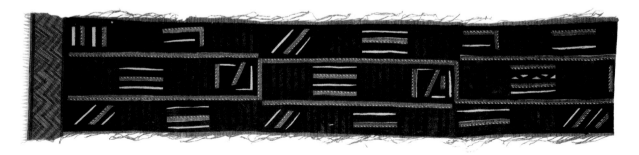

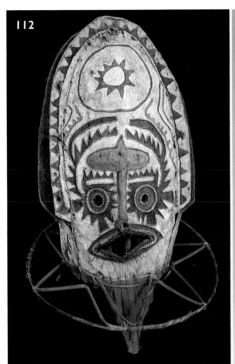

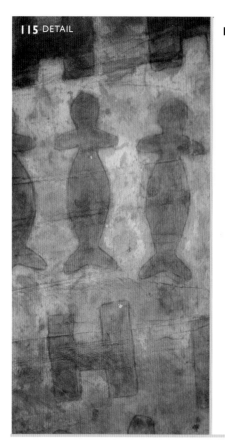

115 DETAIL

116

118

119

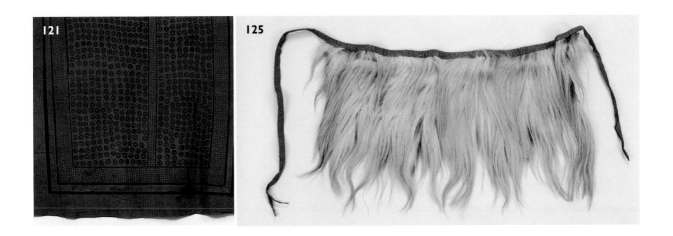

121

125

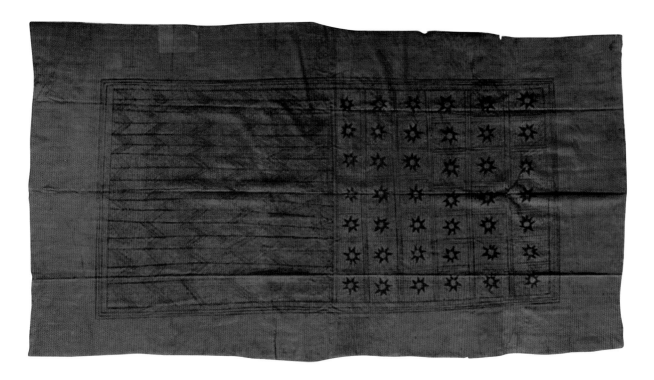

122

126

128

130

129

131 (FOR DETAIL SEE BACK INSIDE COVER)

133

134

135

136

137

138

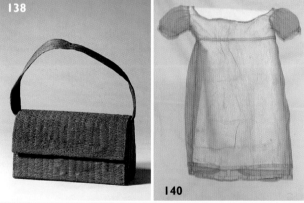

140

141

139

10 | Catalogue captions

Catalogue No.	Museum No.	Caption
( ) : not illustrated		O : origin D : dimensions in millimeters C : collector / donor (*donor unless otherwise stated*)
I	738/1997	Used in association with blowpipe darts, this gourd contains a nerve poison, probably a *Strychnos bisindole* alkaloid, named 'calabash curare' because it is stored in gourds. Death is caused by respiratory paralysis. Curare can remain active for many years, even in its dried state, as here. Collected before 1866. O Amazon region, south America D Ht. 60 Dia: 102 C Probably Searle
2	9/1889/109	Sample of bark from an unidentified tree from the Lower Congo, collected in the 1870s. It was said to have been used as a 'test' in an ordeal. O Lower Congo, central Africa D L. 311 W. 118 C Dennett
(3)	606/1974/1	Coat, *attush*, Ainu people, Japan. Clothing, *amip*, of elm bark cloth, *attush*, was made on a full size loom. Sometimes indigo-dyed cotton thread was added to the warp. The design was appliquéd using cotton cloth cut from old Japanese *kimono* or from old bed covers, with embroidery in couched thread. Acquired before 1896. O Ishicari district, Hokkaido, Japan D L. 1180 W. 1300 C Little

Catalogue No.	Museum No.	Caption
( ) : not illustrated		O : origin D : dimensions in millimeters C : collector / donor (*donor unless otherwise stated*)
(4)	606/1974/2	Apron, *attush*, Ainu people, Japan. Cloth of elm bark fibre and cotton, with embroidered indigo appliqué. The designs contain elements believed to ward off evil spirits. Acquired in the Ishicari district of Hokkaido from Ainu fishermen before 1896.
		O Ishicari district, Hokkaido, Japan D L. 590 W(inc.ties) 1863 C Little
5	LN. 24/11/03/5	Cedar bark strip, given by a member of the Na-yii family group from Vancouver Island who came with Tim Paul to create *Ilchinik* the totem pole now in the World Cultures gallery, in 1998.
		O Nuu-chah-nulth Nation, Northwest Coast, north America D Ht. 130; L. 295; W. 250 C Burkinshaw loan
6	E772	Whalebone bark mallet, used to beat the inner bark of cedar on a large flat pebble. Collected between 1863 and 1866.
		O Northwest Coast, north America. D L. 270 C Gregory
(7)	255/1998	Headband of cedar bark worn on ceremonial occasions; (unfinished), given as for no 5.
		O Nuu-chah-nulth Nation, Northwest Coast, north America D Dia. 240 C Jane Burkinshaw
8	176/2000	Headband of cedar bark, worn on ceremonial occasions; given as for no 5.
		O Nuu-chah-nulth Nation, Northwest Coast, north America D L. 433 C Len Pole
9	E797	Cedar bark cape, worn by high-ranking people; originally edged in sea otter fur. Acquired by Agassiz at Cape Flattery, Washington Sate, USA, as First Lieutenant on HMS *America* in 1845.
		O Makah Nation, Northwest Coast, north America D W. 1760; D. 1169 C Agassiz

Catalogue No.	Museum No.	Caption
( ) : not illustrated		O : origin D : dimensions in millimeters C : collector / donor (donor unless otherwise stated)
10	70/1927/9	Basket, the base made of cedar bark in plain weave. The sides are wrapped over slanting verticals. Collected in the late-19th or early-20th century by Edgar Dewdney.
		O Nuu-chah-nulth Nation, Northwest Coast, north America D L. 173; W. 120; Ht. 75 C Dewdney
(11)	70/1927/11	Basket with a base of red cedar bark strips in plain weave, which have been split to form the verticals of the sides. Collected in the late-19th or early-20th century by Edgar Dewdney.
		O Nuu-chah-nulth Nation, Northwest Coast, north America D L. 70 C Dewdney
12	70/1227/6	Basket of cedar root with an imbricated decoration in cherry bark. The geometric design represents butterflies. Made in the early-19th century. Collected in the late-19th or early-20th century by Edgar Dewdney.
		O Salish Nation, Fraser River region, Northwest Coast, north America. D L. 405 C Dewdney
13	70/1927/7	Basket of cedar root with an imbricated decoration in cherry bark. The holes in the rim show that straps were attached for carrying the basket slung on the back. Collected in the late-19th or early-20th century by Edgar Dewdney.
		O Salish Nation, Northwest Coast, north America D L. 480 C Dewdney
14	249/1905	Hat of tamarind bark strips in imitation of a European form; late-19th century.
		O Antigua, West Indies D L. 396; W. 340; Ht. 135 C Miss Hainworth

Catalogue No.	Museum No.	Caption
( ) : not illustrated		O : origin D : dimensions in millimeters C : collector / donor (*donor unless otherwise stated*)
(15)	samples	Samples of cords of bark strips. There are different types of *cipó* fibre (*Philodendron sp., Connarus sp. or Heteropsis sp.*) which are used in various ways. The bark can be stripped from the wood, scraped and used in woven objects. These samples are from Museu do Indio, Rio de Janeiro. The worked sample of *envira* (*Guatteria sp.*) or *cipó*, could be a binding from a weapon. It has a residue of a coating of resin on it. O Amazon region, south America. D L. (average)1225 C Collector: Carvalho
16	11/1900/55	Arrow with bark bindings. Arrow with a unilaterally eight-barbed point, smooth cane shaft and inner-bark fibre strip bindings. The shaped quill and folded top of the feather are fixed to the shaft with the bindings. Collected before 1900. O Amazon region, south America. D L. 1450 C Peek
17	11/1900/141	Bow. Flat-back, convex-belly cross-sectioned bow of un-smoothed dark hardwood. There are inner-bark strip bindings in the middle and at both ends, incorporating red feathers at one end. Collected before 1900. O Amazon region, south America D L. 1880 C Peek
18	E992/5	Blowpipe, made of a split single tube bound together along its entire length with the inner bark of the liane vine or *envira* (*Guatteria sp.*). The mouthpiece is made of bone. For hunting birds and monkeys, and other small mammals for food. Collected before 1866. O Amazon region, south America D L. 2743 C Searle
19	11/1900/1	Water tube or flute of a length of bamboo, with bark bindings. Documented as a 'water tube', this object was collected from the Botocudo people. However, it may be a flute, with part of the mouthpiece missing. Collected before 1900. O Rio Doce, Brazil. D L. 1198 C Peek

Catalogue No.	Museum No.	Caption
( ) : not illustrated		O : origin D : dimensions in millimeters C : collector / donor (donor unless otherwise stated)
20	138/2000/9	Bag with straps made of *envira* bark in an open-weave style made by many Amazonian groups. This one may be from the Maku or Yanomami people. Probably made in the 19th century. O Amazon region, south America. D Ht. 740; W. 284 C Unknown
21	105/2003/24	A temporary or disposable burden basket woven from *buriti* fibre strips with a strap of *envira* inner bark from the second stage of processing. Collected in 2003. O Kayapo people, Amazon region, south America. D Ht. 610 C Collector: Carvalho
22	33/1953/48	Bag for glass spearheads, collected from Wyndam in the Kimberley range; late-19th century. O Kimberley, Western Australia. D L. 260; W. 75 C Lt-Col. Montague
23	9/1895/2	Canoe of birch bark, said to have been built at Thunder Bay 'for the late Mr Harry Burrows of Teignmouth' Given to the museum in 1895. O Mi'kmaq, eastern woodlands region, north America D L. 3910; W. 750 C Capt Corder
24	E755	Birchbark canoe model with dyed quill decoration. The edges are layered with white quill and bound with birch strips sewn onto the body of the canoe. Quill decoration is not documented on any full-sized Mi'kmaq canoes. Collected before 1877. O Mi'kmaq, eastern woodlands region, north America D L. 520; W. 74 C Grant
25	E748	A round box made of birchbark with undyed or dyed but faded porcupine quill floral design on the lid. It can be dated to the early-19th century, as the later Mi'kmaq work was more brilliantly coloured. Collected before 1873. O Mi'kmaq, eastern woodlands region, north America. D Dia. 70; Ht. 67 C Bowring

Catalogue No.	Museum No.	Caption
( ) : not illustrated		O : origin D : dimensions in millimeters C : collector / donor (donor unless otherwise stated)
26	70/1927/15	Birch bark container, with rim bindings of birch root or perhaps cherry bark. The design is made by scraping away the dark inner bark to expose the layer of light bark beneath. Acquired by Edgar Dewdney after 1879. O Possibly Ojibwe (Chippeway), north America. D L. 180: W.100 C Dewdney
27	12/1935	Container of two layers of birch bark, made in two pieces, the lid to slide over the case. Embroidery in dyed moose hair, with a design on one side of two sets of two pipe-smoking figures, and long-tailed birds in trees. The other side has a pair of figures and one single figure. Probably made about 1850. O Wyandot (Huron), north America. D Ht. 133; W. 73 C Seaward
28	212/1996/16	Box lid of birchbark, embroidered with dyed porcupine quill. Probably made in the early-19 century. O Mi'kmaq, north America. D L.268; W. 167 C Unknown
(29)	70/1927/22	Picture frame of birch bark, embroidered with dyed quillwork of flower sprays. Said to be of Sioux origin. O north America D Ht.162; w.130 C Dewdney
30	219/1996/4	Painting of fish on paper mounted on board. Painted by Liwukan, Cape York and purchased in the mid-1970s. O Cape York Peninsula, Queensland, Australia D Ht. 510; W. 410 C Tanner

Catalogue No.	Museum No.	Caption
( ) : not illustrated		O : origin D : dimensions in millimeters C : collector / donor (donor unless otherwise stated)
(31)	75/1951/2/2 and LN 15/12/03/3	Tobacco pipe of cherry wood, with case and pouch of cherry bark. O Japan D Case: L.241; W.270 C Bourne, and loan by National Trust, Snowshill Manor
(32)	E499	Shi-bachi, a fire box with cork covering. The upper box is used to contain the live charcoal, the drawers the tobacco. Collected before 1872. O Japan D L.215; W.152; Ht.165 C Perkins
(33)	sample	Samples of cork from Quercus suber, showing the outer bark as it comes from the tree, panels of boiled bark and flattened bark sheets from which corks are punched. O Portugal D C Kindly supplied by Rankins Brothers & Sons.
34	127/2001/14/1,2	Section of branch and the bark as it comes off the tree. Purchased in February 2001. O Fatu Hiva, Marquesas Islands D L.385mm C Collector: Balfour-Paul
35	127/2001/12	Tool for prising bark off a tree. Purchased in February 2001. O Fatu Hiva, Marquesas Islands D L.252 C Collector: Balfour-Paul
36	127/2001/11	Wood beater with grooves on two sides. Purchased in February 2001. O Fatu Hiva, Marquesas Islands D L.350; W.40 C Collector: Balfour-Paul
37	127/2001/14/3	Mulberry bark after first beating. Purchased in February 2001. O Fatu Hiva, Marquesas Islands D 432 × 66 C Collector: Balfour-Paul

Catalogue No.	Museum No.	Caption
( ) : not illustrated		O : origin D : dimensions in millimeters C : collector / donor (*donor unless otherwise stated*)
38	127/2001/9	Plain mulberry bark cloth sample. Purchased in February 2001. O Fatu Hiva, Marquesas Islands D 770 x 510 C Collector: Balfour-Paul
39	127/2001/13	Fine brush of human hair used for painting designs on barkcloth. Purchased in February 2001. O Fatu Hiva, Marquesas Islands D L.130 C Collector: Balfour-Paul
40	LN 4/04/03.1	Book of barkcloth samples published by Alexander Shaw in 1787, consisting of an introduction and 39 samples – 20 from Tahiti, 14 from Hawaii, four from Tonga and one from Jamaica. O Tahiti, Hawaii, Tonga, Jamaica. D L.225; W.190 C Private loan
41	E1767e	Fragmentary piece of thick, very dark brown cloth, showing no beater marks. O Tahiti D L.1235; W. 320 C Bond/Devon & Exeter Institution
(42)	59/1994/12/ 9-12	Fragments of cloth, possibly some of the pieces mentioned in the accession register as coming from the Devon & Exeter Institution therefore associated with the Bond collection. No. 9 has a red edge, all are otherwise undecorated which suggests an early post-European contact date. O Tahiti D 274 x 215; 315 x 275; 295 x 230; 475 x 230 C possibly Bond/Devon & Exeter Institution
43	E1767b	Cape (*'ahu-fara*), a rectangle of off-white cloth showing yellow pigment in some areas. A piece of fine black barkcloth applied to the centre area. It has scissor cut indents, and sets of V cuts in two rectangles revealing red barkcloth underlay. There are fern printed designs around the border, and some on the underside. Transferred to the Museum from the DEI in 1868; D'Alleva comments of this cloth "stylistically related to a barkcloth in the

Catalogue No.	Museum No.	Caption
( ) : not illustrated		O : origin D : dimensions in millimeters C : collector / donor (donor unless otherwise stated)
		British Museum, collected by the Providence's midshipman, Matthew Flinders, and to the mourning dress cape" (cat no. 45) (D'Alleva, 1995, p.40).
		O Tahiti D W.1776;D.1290 C Bond/Devon & Exeter Institution
44	E1767c	Loincloth (maro or fa'aio), a long thin section of cloth with red rubbed pigment on one surface. Collection history as for cat no. 39. D'Alleva comments that this 'resembles a type of loincloth worn by initiates to the Arioi society' (D'Alleva, 1995, p.41).
		O Tahiti D 2600 × 830 C Bond/Devon & Exeter Institution
45	E1776-1781	Costume of a chief mourner at the funeral of a high class noble in Tahiti, a Polynesian Island in the Pacific Ocean. The cape ('ahu-fara) is made of barkcloth, the poncho (tiputa) of barkcloth and coconut shell discs, the chest apron of slivers of pearl shell, the breast-plate of wood and pearl shell, the headpiece of pearl shell and feathers of the Tropic Bird, the turban of barkcloth and matting. The costume was used in the 18th century during funerals of kings and nobles. Such costumes also served as high status gifts for officers on Cook's and Bligh's voyages, after they ceased to be used in funerals.
		O Tahiti D Ht. 1890; W. 850 C Bond/Devon & Exeter Institution
46	E1736	Wooden beater with four incised surfaces, three with parallel grooves of different thick-nesses, one with a grid of lines, an unusual feature on beaters from Tahiti. Presented to the Devon & Exeter Institution, between 1813 and about 1825, by Capt Bond.
		O Tahiti D L. 340 C Bond/Devon & Exeter Institution
47	Loan B80	Cape; a rectangle of off-white cloth decorated with fern print motifs and edges painted red on three sides. Probably acquired in the 1830s.
		O Tahiti D W. 2275; D.1340 C Bandinel loan

Catalogue No.	Museum No.	Caption
( ) : not illustrated		O : origin D : dimensions in millimeters C : collector / donor (donor unless otherwise stated)
48	10/1949/1&2	Skirt and headdress of a dance costume: the headdress is made of a band of barkcloth with vegetable fibre rosettes. Part of a dance costume. Collected before 1949.
		O Tahiti D Dia. 230 C Mrs Gould
49	51/1916/ 141, 142	Plain rectangles of cloth, showing fold lines.
		O Pitcairn D 1225 x 1115 C George Peard
50	E1252	Poncho (tiputa), black painted rectangle in centre, surrounded by light brown, tan and dark brown lines. Made before 1867. The accession register entry is confusing as to the provenance of this piece, making reference both to 'Hervey islands' (Cook Islands) and to the general statement that 'bark of paper mulberry is used by the Sandwich Islanders'. Tiputa of this form were worn in the Cook Islands but the decoration is unusual for this archipelago.
		O Cook Islands D L.2179; W.630 C Mrs Norrington
51	E1263	Large rectangle of cloth with smooth white surface; central panel of black toothed triangles and millipede-like creatures with jaws at each end and five-fingered legs, border of brick-wall bands and zig-zag lines. The piece was collected during the Cook voyages, but without any clear indication as to where it was made or what the startling designs signify.
		The fact of its decoration is itself worthy of comment even though the meaning of the motifs is unknown. As Kaeppler has suggested, the items which Cook himself acquired, the great majority of which went to the Leverian Museum, were of a high status origin and a ceremonial purpose (Kaeppler, 1978a:18). It is clear from a number of sources that high status barkcloth in Tahiti and elsewhere in central Polynesia at the time of the earliest European contact was plain and white. This piece is therefore unusual in being highly decorated in a very distinctive way. The nearest parallels to its decorative style are a small number of cloths, one formerly in the Hooper collection, another in Kew, a third in the British Museum

Catalogue No.	Museum No.	Caption
( ) : not illustrated		O : origin D : dimensions in millimeters C : collector / donor (donor unless otherwise stated)

(Kooijman, 1972: 59) and other examples in the Bishop Museum and Vienna (illustrated in Kaeppler, 1978b:164). Each of these is frustratingly short on original documentation.
The ex-Hooper piece is said to have come from Tongataboo before 1833 (Phelps, 1976:163). Only the Exeter piece is assignable to a Cook voyage origin, and even here there is room for some doubt.

Other examples showing a similar style of decoration are associated with Cook Islands staff gods, including the well-known piece in the British Museum (Barrow, 1979:85; Meyer,1995:523). This is from the London Missionary Society collection, and therefore associated with the destruction of the objects with traditional Rarotongan religious connections, initiated by Revd John Williams in the 1820s. The total length of the staff is 396 cm and the lower edge of the decorated cloth in which the central section is wrapped has precisely the same 'brick wall' designs as on the Exeter piece. Compare also the man's waistband in the Royal Museum of Scotland, also from Rarotonga (Idiens, 1990:53). These similarities need to be investigated in relation to the other staff gods, such those in Auckland (Neich & Pendergrast, 1997:77), Dunedin (Meyer, 1995:522), and the Bishop Museum, Honolulu, with barkcloth wrappings exhibiting closely related design motifs. This idea was first put forward by Kooijman (1972:56-60), but dismissed by Kaeppler (Kaeppler, 1978b:160). The notion that the Cook voyage cloth in Exeter is from the Cook Islands is on the face of it unlikely since he did not set foot there on any of his voyages. A brief landing was made at Atiu (Kaeppler,1978b:165) in 1777 but Cook himself did not disembark. No Cook Island (Rarotonga or Mangaia) staff gods appear in collections before the ravages of Revd Williams in the early 1820s. There are therefore a number of difficulties in the confident association of this barkcloth to a Cook Islands (Rarotonga) provenance. However, Kooijman assembles a good case for assigning this category of decorated cloth to such an origin (even though he was unfortunately not aware of the existence of this particular piece in 1972), mostly from small examples in the Peabody Museum Harvard, Field Museum Chicago and the Bishop Museum. This contention now needs urgent and comprehensive re-examination, particularly in the context of the extensive central Polynesian trade networks which existed immediately before the earliest European contact.

O Probably Cook Islands D L.5300 W.1780 C Collected by James Cook, given by James Vaughan.

Catalogue No.	Museum No.	Caption
( ) : not illustrated		O : origin D : dimensions in millimeters C : collector / donor (*donor unless otherwise stated*)
52	240/1914	Wood beater, each face incised with grooves of differing degrees of fineness. Collected by Vice Admiral Leah when he was Commander of the Mildura in the Pacific in 1894.
		O Cook Islands D L.366 C Leah
53	127/2001/1	Piece of cloth made from Mulberry bark, with a turtle design. Collected in February 2001.
		O Fatu Hiva, Marquesas Islands D 767 × 548 C Collector: Balfour-Paul
54	127/2001/2	Piece of cloth made from Banyan bark, depicting eyes of the '*tiki*' human figure. The design is signed 'D. Eve'. Collected in February 2001.
		O Fatu Hiva, Marquesas Islands D 380 × 255 C Collector: Balfour-Paul
55	127/2001/3	Piece of cloth made from banyan bark, with a *tiki* human figure design and a border of solid black triangles. Collected in February 2001.
		O Fatu Hiva, Marquesas Islands D 340 × 207 C Collector: Balfour-Paul
56	127/2001/4	Piece of cloth made from breadfruit tree root with geometric and curvilinear designs. Collected in February 2001.
		O Fatu Hiva, Marquesas Islands D 494 × 238 C Collector: Balfour-Paul
57	127/2001/5	Piece of cloth made from breadfruit bark, with geometric designs. Collected in February 2001.
		O Fatu Hiva, Marquesas Islands D 444 × 234 C Collector: Balfour-Paul
58	127/20001/6	Piece of cloth made from banyan bark, with a turtle design. Collected in February 2001.
		O Fatu Hiva, Marquesas Islands D 429 × 314 C Collector: Balfour-Paul

Catalogue No.	Museum No.	Caption
( ) : not illustrated		O : origin D : dimensions in millimeters C : collector / donor (*donor unless otherwise stated*)
59	127/20001/7	Piece of cloth made from mulberry bark, with geometric designs on yellow from turmeric. Collected in February 2001.
		O Fatu Hiva, Marquesas Islands D 161 × 115 C Collector: Balfour-Paul
60	127/20001/8	Plain glazed mulberry barkcloth. Collected in February 2001.
		O Fatu Hiva, Marquesas Islands D 407 × 285 C Collector: Balfour-Paul
61	E1734	Wood beater, early-19th century, incised with crosshatched lines which only feature on Hawaiian beaters. Like the Hawaiian piece of barkcloth, cat no.71, this is incorrectly indicated in the original register as having been collected by Capt Bond.
		O Hawaii D L.355; W.30 C Devon & Exeter Institution
62	E1735	Wood beater, early-19th century. Presented to the Devon & Exeter institution, probably before about 1825, from an unknown donor.
		O Hawaii D L.355; W.30 C Devon & Exeter Institution
63	59/2000/2-7	Bamboo stamps for use in decorating barkcloth.
		O Hawaii D L. 439, 420, 383, 377, 371, 336. C Wakeham
64	VS 1515	Design of squares with 10-pointed stars made by use of stamp. Said by the donor to have been called 'Wauti' (*wauke* is the name for the paper mulberry in Hawaii).
		O Honolulu, Hawaii D 2190 × 1100 C Lang

Catalogue No.	Museum No.	Caption
( ) : not illustrated		O : origin D : dimensions in millimeters C : collector / donor (donor unless otherwise stated)
65 **66** **67** **(68)** **(69)** **(70)** **71**	58/1994/1-6,8	Fragments, probably early-19th century. It is possible that these pieces are the same as those referred to in the museum's accession register as '7 small pieces of tapa cloth' presented by the Devon & Exeter Institution, in 1868, museum number E1768. Although these were said to be from 'Otaheite, Atuoi, etc.', no other items in the museum can be linked to this accession. O Hawaii D 310 x 248; 485 x 175; 448 x 183; 180 x 80; 215 x 71; 156 x 72; 590 x 350 C Unknown donor (possibly associated with the Devon & Exeter Institution)
72	E1767a	Long rectangle with a small square cut from one long side. Decorated in stripes of fine zig-zag lines. This piece is associated with the items collected by Bond in Tahiti, but is Hawaiian. Together with 12 other pieces of barkcloth, supposedly from Tahiti, it was acquired by the museum from the Devon & Exeter Institution in 1868 and said to have been presented by Capt Bond. Either this piece was collected by him on Tahiti, or has incorrectly been associated with the Bond pieces (see also the barkcloth beater cat no. 61), possibly from another collector who presented Hawaiian items to the Institution. O Hawaii D 1370 x 424 C Bond/Devon & Exeter Institution
73	59/2000/1	Book of samples, mostly fragments from Hawaii coloured with modern dyes but the largest piece is probably Tongan. O Hawaii D W.259; L.183 C Wakeham
74	59/1994/3	Rectangle of cloth cut from a larger piece. Individual motifs have been produced using kupesi rubbing boards, including clover leaf, star, crescent moon, lines of triangles, outlined in dark lines, within panels. O Tonga D L.3540; W1950 C Unknown

Catalogue No.	Museum No.	Caption
( ) : not illustrated		O : origin D : dimensions in millimeters C : collector / donor (donor unless otherwise stated)
75	102/1949/4	Rectangle cut from a larger piece. Bands of motifs in black, and a repeated label PAPEMAKAIKOTOGO with a rubbed ground in brown. Collected before 1949. O Tonga D L. 3780; W. 1750 C Elliott
76	54/2003/3	Fragment of cloth with rubbed design, plus outlined diamonds, triangles and dog? Mid-19th century; collector unknown. O Tonga? D 1060 × 925 C Transferred from the Burton Art Gallery, Bideford
77	7/1983/3a	Square cloth with a pattern of diamonds and triangles with a solid. Acquired by Mrs Cudmore at the same time as cat no. 78. O Tonga D Sq. 735 C Cudmore
78	7/1983/3b	Square cloth with the Tongan coat of arms, a cross within a six-pointed star, with crossed swords, stars, birds and a crown. The banners below bear the letters KOE OTUA, MO TONGA KONO, KU TOFIA. This cloth was made for Mrs Cudmore by her Tongan Red Cross colleagues on her departure from the islands in 1975. The central coat of arms is similar to that illustrated as a *kupesi* rubbing board in Neich & Pendergrast 1997:57, see also Kooijman, 1972:340. O Tonga D Sq. 895 C Cudmore
79	7/1983/11	Fan with barkcloth backing. Acquired by the donor in 1975. O Tonga D L. 391; W. 300 C Cudmore

Catalogue No.	Museum No.	Caption
( ) : not illustrated		O : origin D : dimensions in millimeters C : collector / donor (*donor unless otherwise stated*)
80	E1899	Rectangle of cloth with a hand painted design of opposed black triangles on a ground of a faint netted pattern. Collected before 1878. Said to have been made on Tutuila, but some of the design elements are more closely associated with the Cakaudrove area of Fiji. O Tutuila, Samoa D 2610 × 1450 C Coumbe
81	E1898	Rectangle of cloth cut from a larger piece, with rubbed designs, no overpainting. Collected before 1878. O Upolu, Samoa. D 1920 × 1240 C Coumbe
82	73/1999/1	Rectangle of cloth, *siapo tasina*, with rubbed designs elements of which have been overpainted in dark brown in a regular sequence. O Samoa D 1550 × 1310 C Bosence
83	E1900	Rectangular cloth with rubbed designs almost obliterated by hand painted designs heavily varnished using resin from the *o'a* tree. Made before 1878. Said to have been 'used as a native dress by wrapping round the loins'. O Tutuila, Samoa D 2200 × 1400 C Coumbe
84	367/1914	Panelled design made with the use of a wooden design board, some of the motifs outlined. Collected before 1914. O Samoa D 1710 × 1860 C Major W. H. Collins

Catalogue No.	Museum No.	Caption
( ) : not illustrated		O : origin D : dimensions in millimeters C : collector / donor (donor unless otherwise stated)

85 — 129/1972/29

A cloth bearing a version of the common 'vane swastika' motif, consisting of triangles arranged within a square. This piece was collected by the Marriotts between 1878 and 1904.

O Samoa D 1870 × 1405 C Collector: Revd John Marriott. Donor: Hooper

86 — 18/1962/1

A cloth with a bold and unusual design thought to be from Samoa. Made before 1962.

O Probably Samoa D 1604 × 1060 C Knill

87 — 80/1928

A cloth of Samoan origin which was said to have been made in New Zealand. It has a typical Samoan pattern of the 'vane swastika' type alternating with narrow leaflets. Made before 1928.

O Samoa D 1880 × 1315 C Miss Heroine

88 — 129/1972/31

A poncho or *tiputa* made from a piece of cloth with a traditional design built up of sets of narrow leaflets. The *tiputa* was introduced to Samoa by European missionaries from Tahiti in the 1830s. This piece was collected between 1878 and 1904.

O Samoa D L.1550; W.670 C Collector: Revd John Marriott. Donor: Hooper

89 — 59/2000/33

Oval table cover with border of deeply cut lined triangles and floral motifs. This is an adaptation for the tourist market. The item was collected in Hawaii, but the style suggests it may have been made on Tutuila in American Samoa. .

O Probably Samoa D 1110 × 930 C Wakeham

90 — 54/2003/2

Oval mat with concentric curvilinear designs. The origin of this piece has not been clearly established.

O Probably Samoa D 1000 × 850 C Transferred from the Burton Art Gallery, Bideford

Catalogue No.	Museum No.	Caption
( ) : not illustrated		**O** : origin **D** : dimensions in millimeters **C** : collector / donor (*donor unless otherwise stated*)
(91)	18/1962/2	Whip. An example of the unconventional uses to which bark and barkcloth have been put, usually under European influence. Collected before 1962.
		O Fiji or Samoa. **D** L.1352 **C** Mrs Knill
92	129/1972/25	Poncho (*tiputa*) leaflet designs applied freehand, some of them subsequently filled in with purple pigment at some time between the period of acquisition by the Marriotts (1878-1904) and their acquisition by the museum in 1972.
		O Uvea (Wallis Island) **D** L. 1120; W. 510 **C** Collector: Revd Marriott. Donor: Hooper
93	129/1972/26	Poncho (*tiputa*). Designs applied using a rubbing board; some of the motifs have been filled in with purple and/or yellow pigment at some time between the period of acquisition by the Marriotts (1878-1904) and their acquisition by the museum in 1972.
		O Uvea (Wallis Island) **D** L. 960; W. 480 **C** Collector: Revd Marriott. Donor: Hooper
94	54/2003/8	Large rectangular cloth with lined designs similar to some associated with Niue Island.
		O Probably Niue **D** 3600 x 3550 **C** Transferred from the Burton Art Gallery, Bideford
95	129/1972/28	Small irregular piece with panels of diamonds and border of sets of leaflets.
		O Niue or Samoa **D** 1600 x 1150 **C** Collector: Revd John Marriott. Donor: Hooper

Catalogue No.	Museum No.	Caption
( ) : not illustrated		O : origin D : dimensions in millimeters C : collector / donor (*donor unless otherwise stated*)

96 VS1516 *Masi vulavula*: all white, very finely beaten, with small overlap triangles as a decorative feature. Edges have been cut on three sides into hangers, at an acute angle at the sides, straight at the lower edge. The cloth has been sharply folded in concertina form. Originally accessioned as a sample of a vegetable substance with the description: 'Broussonetia papyrifera, cloth from bark. Feejee islands. Very fine and white' Acquired by the museum in 1879, from Isaac Lang, a grain and seed merchant in Okehampton Street, Exeter.

O Fiji D 1240 x 770 C Lang

97 59/1994/5 *Masi kesa*: Long rectangle of cloth decorated in black and red with a deep stencilled border, black patterned infills and white rectangles including stencilled rosettes. One long edge is cut into angled hangers.

O Fiji D L. 4235; W. 1225 C Unknown donor

98 202/1978/3 *Masi kesa*: Rectangle of cloth with stencilled patterns; one end serrated. Collected before 1978.

O Fiji D L. 2520; W. 760 C Mrs Taylor

99 E1904 *Masi kesa*: Rectangle of cloth, built up using a range of stencilled motifs, and blocks of freehand triangles in black with occasional red line markings delineating the boundary of some pattern areas. Collected before 1879.

O Fiji D L. 2860; W. 1300 C Donor: Isaac Lang. Brought to England by James Lang

100 54/2003/5 *Masi kesa*: Rectangle of cloth with panels of stencilled designs including rosettes. Mid-19th century; collector unknown.

O Fiji D L. 3600; W. 900 C Transferred from the Burton Art Gallery, Bideford

Catalogue No.	Museum No.	Caption
( ) : not illustrated		O : origin D : dimensions in millimeters C : collector / donor (*donor unless otherwise stated*)
101	815/1997/1	*Masi kesa*: Rectangle of cloth, built up using a range of stencilled motifs. This piece was said to have been made by nursing graduates who had been taught by the donor's aunt in the 1970s. O Fiji D L. 3772; W. 625 C Kempson
102	73/1999/2	*Masi kesa*: Rectangle of cloth built up using a range of stencilled motifs. It was probably made in the 1970s, certainly before 1985, when it was illustrated in Susan Bosence's book *Hand Block Printing and Resist Dyeing*. O Probably Taveuni, Fiji D L.1490; W.1120 C Bosence
103	54/2003/1	Skirt in European style, made up of a piece of barkcloth with a waistband of stencilled designs. Mid-19th century; collector unknown. O Fiji D L.790 C Transferred from the Burton Art Gallery, Bideford
104	202/1978/2	*Masi kesa*: Rectangle of cloth, with stencilled motifs similar to those illustrated in Kooijman from the Island of Mothe (Kooijiman, 1988:40). Collected before 1978. O Mothe, Lau Islands, Fiji. D L. 2710; W. 800 C Mrs Taylor
105	54/2003/4	Long rectangle of cloth with a deep border built up of stencilled motifs. Decorated with long diamonds in the Cakaudrove style and ladder motifs in red. It has been cut from a much larger piece. Mid-19th century; collector unknown. O Cakaudrove district, Vanua Levu, Fiji D L. 5600; W. 1400 C Transferred from the Burton Art Gallery

Catalogue No.	Museum No.	Caption
( ) : not illustrated		O : origin D : dimensions in millimeters C : collector / donor (*donor unless otherwise stated*)

106 E1905 Large cloth of panels of diamond designs. This is an example of the kind of cloth design and size called *taunamu* by Neich & Pendergrast (1997:115-7) meaning 'mosquito guard'. Used as a room divider. Collected before 1879.

O Probably Moala island, Fiji D L. 3796; W. 3640 C Donor: Isaac Lang. Brought to England by James Lang

107 Loan M44 Rubbing board (*kupeti*), made of pandanus leaves with stitched line designs. This form of board was of Tongan origin.

O Fiji D L. 530; W. 160 C Maidstone Museum loan

108 815/1997/2 Cloth with rubbed design showing use of the rubbing board with no added design; late-19th century.

O Fiji D L. 1100; W. 830 C Kempson

109 48/1916 Rectangular cloth, part of a much larger piece. Made in a Tongan style, probably from the Lau Islands, with designs of frigate birds and union jacks with dark brown dots interspersed in the design. The union jack design has been produced using a rubbing board. The cloth was presented to the Governor of the Fiji islands in 1902 'by one of the native chiefs'. It was said that 'such cloths were used as carpets for the chief and his suite upon ceremonial occasions'. Another portion of the cloth was given to the Victoria & Albert Museum.

O Probably Lau Islands, Fiji D L. 5340; W. 2780 C Lady Sargood

110 E2021 Long rectangle of cloth with dark cross-hatched sections possibly made using a bamboo roller. The design is similar to a piece in the Brenchley collection, collected on the same voyage (see Section 8). Made before 1865. Collected on the voyage of the *Curaçoa* in 1865.

O Possibly from Viti Levu, Fiji D L.3080; W. 618 C Collector: John Gould Veitch

Catalogue No.	Museum No.	Caption
( ) : not illustrated		O : origin D : dimensions in millimeters C : collector / donor (*donor unless otherwise stated*)
(111)	Loan M 18(395)	Cloth similar to cat no.110. Collected on the voyage of the *Curaçoa* in 1865.
		O Fiji D L.3200;W.680 C Maidstone Museum loan, ex. Brenchley
112	88/1938/1	Mask, called *eharo*, made from rattan and beaten bark stretched over a wooden frame. The mask represents a mythical being and is worn during dance ceremonies. After the ceremonies have concluded these masks are discarded. Collected before 1938.
		O Purari delta, Papua New Guinea D Ht.750;W. 350 C Purchased Stevens Auction
113	810/1997/1	Rectangle of cloth with red and black freehand designs. Given to a member of the New Guinea mission, stationed at St Barnabas Hospital, Dogura, in about 1973.
		O Probably Oro Province, South-East Papua New Guinea. D L.1290;W. 560 C Bradbrook
114	E1693	Mask; wood face with barkcloth hair piece. Made before 1877.
		O New Ireland D Ht. 230;W. 220; D. 280 C Thomson
115	Loan M42	Cream coloured rectangle decorated with H-shaped motifs and fish rendered in indigo blue outlined in brown. Collected by Julius Brenchley from Santa Isabel in 1865.
		O Santa Isabel, Solomon Islands. D L.1520 C Maidstone Museum loan
116	38/1998	Square of cloth with black painted designs. Each design has a specific meaning, relating to a traditional custom or belief. Made by Matthias Melikeva in Nea village, Ndende' Santa Cruz in 1996.
		O Ndende Island, Santa Cruz D 280 × 285 C Blaylock

Catalogue No.	Museum No.	Caption
( ) : not illustrated		O : origin D : dimensions in millimeters C : collector / donor (donor unless otherwise stated)
(117)	LN 15/12/03/1	Rectangle of cloth with panels of black hatched lines. Made in 2002.
		O Ndende Island, Santa Cruz D 850 × 270 C Sherry Doyal loan
118	292/1914	Rectangle of cloth. Used in gifts associated with marriage ceremonies; also worn draped over the shoulder by women for ceremonial display. Collected by Commander Leah of the Cruiser *Mildura* while in the Pacific in1894.
		O Erromango, Vanuatu D 1630 × 860 C Leah
119	1069/1988	Sleeveless jacket of brown barkcloth, trimmed with red and black trade cloth. Collected by an Australian soldier in about 1946 from the Dayak area of inland Kalimantan.
		O Kalimantan, Borneo D L. 660; W. 440-490 C Frazer
(120)	LN.24/11/03/4.1	Plain sheet with beater marks. Made in 1973 by Kwadwo Gyem.
		O Boso, Eastern Region, Ghana D 1460 × 1450 C Len Pole loan
121	35/1929	Large rectangle of cloth, decorated with black motifs within a lined border using lake mud as pigment. This kind of barkcloth was used for ceremonial costume, in decorating the king's palace and as a funeral shroud. Collected by Major Rattray in about 1895.
		O Baganda, Uganda D 3285 × 1920 C Rattray
122	60/1948/110a	Large rectangle of brown cloth with black motifs using lake mud as pigment. Obtained by Col Broun in the 1890s.
		O Baganda, Uganda D 3830 × 2085 C Broun

Catalogue No.	Museum No.	Caption
( ) : not illustrated		O : origin D : dimensions in millimeters C : collector / donor (donor unless otherwise stated)
(123)	LN 24/11/03/3	Busuti; barkcloth dress in European style, with sash and train, made in about 1950.
		O Baganda, Uganda D L. 1340 C Lalage Bown loan
(124)	285/2003/2	Plain rectangle of cloth with raffia sewn repairs. Bought in Kampala in March 2003.
		O Kampala, Uganda D 3260 × 2300 C Kay Pole
125	2/1938/4	Skirt of hide with barkcloth waistband. Collected before 1938.
		O Uganda D L. 2150 (inc ties); D. 525 C Boucher/Leakey
126	67/2002/2	Small round mat, with raffia decoration. Bought in Arusha, northern Tanzania, about 1951.
		O Arusha, Tanzania D Dia.113 C Randall
(127)	LN.24/11/03/2.1	Cushion cover with silk embroidery. Acquired in 2003.
		O Uganda D 375 × 380 C Stephens loan
128	LN.24/11/03/2.2	Cushion cover with applied panel with fish motif. Acquired in 2003.
		O Uganda D 380 × 385 C Stephens loan
129	14/2003	Square of cloth, with patched designs made from Baganda barkcloth. Purchased in 2002.
		O Uganda D 420 × 415 C Purchased 'Something Different', Exeter

Catalogue No.	Museum No.	Caption
( ) : not illustrated		**O** : origin **D** : dimensions in millimeters **C** : collector / donor (*donor unless otherwise stated*)
130	LN.24/11/03/4.2	Bag for coffee, bought in Kampala in March 2003.
		O Uganda **D** Ht. 265, W. 190 **C** Len Pole loan
131	8/1920	Plain brown piece of cloth with clear lattice beater marks. Made by the Azande of Bahr-el-Ghazal province. Collected by A. F. Brown, Conservator of Forests in Sudan, about 1910-20.
		O Bahr El Ghazal, southern Sudan **D** 870 × 464 **C** Brown
(132)	136/1993/46	Plain piece of brown cloth. Early-20th century.
		O Eastern Congo, central Africa. **D** 930 × 269 **C** Transferred from Weston-super-Mare Museum
133 **134**	27/2003/1, 3	*Amate* barkcloth paper with swirling marks, painted birds and flowers, based on local ceramic designs. Probably made in the 1960s by Nahua people.
		O Guerrero, central Mexico **D** Ht.615; W. 212; Ht.615; W.425 **C** Purchased
135	Loan: 24/11/03.1.1	Painted picture on *amate* paper depicting nativity and other village scenes; made by Nahua people. Collected in 2003.
		O Guerrero, central Mexico **D** Ht.588; W.397 **C** Yosi Anaya loan
136	Loan: 24/11/03.1.5	Amate paper with applied figures depicting local gods; made by Otomi people. Collected in 2003.
		O Pahuatl region, central Mexico **D** Ht.615; W.417 **C** Yosi Anaya loan

Catalogue No.	Museum No.	Caption
( ) : not illustrated		O : origin D : dimensions in millimeters C : collector / donor (*donor unless otherwise stated*)
137	E1011	Belt made from two pieces of barkcloth, sewn along the top edge, extending to a twisted tie at each end and joined in the centre by knotted fibre. Painted with a geometric linear and dot design in black with areas of ochre colouring. Collected before 1866.
		O Sarayacu, Amazon D L. 605; D. 60 C Searle
138	LN.15/12/03/1.2	Hand bag with cotton stitching. Bought in Brazil in 2003.
		O Brazil D Ht. 300; W. 270 C Sherry Doyal loan
139	73/1921/74/P	Sample of lace-bark (*Lagetta lagetto*). Collected in the early-20th century.
		O Jamaica D 175 × 85 C Jackson
140	Loan SAFWM 1833.59,60	Child's dress and cap of lace bark, made in 1820s.
		O West Indies D Ht. 680; W. 525 C Saffron Walden Museum loan
141	LN.15/12/03/2	Book of doyley samples, made of lace bark and mountain cabbage palm. Probably made in the mid-19th century and 'Sold for the benefit of the Orphanage for Girls, in Kingston, Jamaica'.
		O Jamaica D 260 × 235 C Horsham Museum loan

11 | References

Author	Year	Title and Publisher	ISBN
Allan, J.	1995	'Artifacts at Exeter City Museums from Bligh's second voyage to Tahiti' in *Pacific Arts*, nos.11, 12:43-47	
Allan, J.	[1996]	*A revised catalogue of the collection of Polynesian artifacts at Exeter City Museums* (Exeter: RAMM archives)	
Anon	1925	*Handbook to the Ethnographic Collections 2nd edition* (London: British Museum)	
Anon	1972	*Peoples and Cultures* (Lisbon: Overseas Museum of Ethnology)	
Anon	1989	*Australian Aboriginal Culture* (Canberra: Australian Government Printing Service)	0644098147
Anaya, Y.	2003	*Notes accompanying acquisition of Mexican barkcloth* (RAMM archives)	
Barrow, T.	1979	*The Art of Tahiti* (London: Thames & Hudson)	050006007
Bosence, S.	1985	*Hand Block Printing and Resist Dyeing* (Newton Abbot: David & Charles)	
Bonnemaison, J. Huffmann, K., et al	1996	*Arts of Vanuatu* (Sydney: Crawford House)	1863331425

Author	Year	Title and Publisher	ISBN
Braun, B. (ed.)	1995	*Arts of the Amazon* (London: Thames & Hudson)	0500278245
Brigham, W. T.	1911	*Ka Hana Kapa* (Honolulu: Bishop Museum)	
Burkinshaw, J.	1999	*Klaya-Ho-Alth: Collections from the Northwest Coast of North America in the Royal Albert Memorial Museum, Exeter* (Exeter City Museums)	1855226952
Carmichael, E. et al	1985	*Hidden Peoples of the Amazon* (London: British Museum)	0714115738
Clark, S.	2003	What's the alternative? in *The Guardian* colour supplement, March 2003.	
Coe, R. T.	1976	*Sacred Circles: Two thousand years of north American Indian art* (London: Arts Council)	01728700964
Cooper, C. et al	1981	*Aboriginal Australia* (Sydney: Australian Gallery Directors Council)	064289689
Craig, B.	1988	*Art & Decoration of Central New Guinea* (Princes Risborough: Shire publications)	0852639414
Cranstone, B.	1961	*Melanesia: A short ethnography* (London: British Museum)	
Cullen, L. P.	1936	'Barkcloth from Africa' in *Natural History*, v.28, no.4	
D'Alleva, A.	1995	'Change and Continuity in Decorated Tahitian barkcloth from Bligh's Second Voyage, 1791-1793' in *Pacific Arts*, nos. 11 & 12: 29-42	
D'Alleva, A.	1998	*Art of the Pacific* (London: Everyman Art Library)	029783617
Danielsson, B., Evrard, M., & Beraud-Villars, M-J.	1972	*La Découverte de la Polynesie* (Paris: Musée de l'Homme)	

Author	Year	Title and Publisher	ISBN
Derbyshire, D.	2000	'Cinnamon may prevent diabetes' (*Daily Telegraph*)	
Diaz, B.	1963	*The Conquest of New Spain* (London: Penguin)	
Edel, M. M.	1957	*Chiga of Western Uganda* (Oxford: IAI/OUP)	
Edge-Partington, J.	1890 -1898	*Ethnographic Album of the Pacific Islands* (Thailand: SDI publications, 1996 reprint)	1878529196
Ellert, H.	1984	*The Material Culture of Zimbabwe* (Zimbabwe: Longman)	
Ellis, W.	1831	*Polynesian Researches* (Vermont: Tuttle, reprint 1969)	0804804753
Ewins, R.	1982	*Fijian Artefacts* (Hobart: Tasmania Museum)	0724610995
Forman, B. M.	1988	*American seating furniture 1630-1730* (London: Norton & Co, London)	
Gathercole, P.	ND [1970]	*'From the Islands of the South Seas 1773-4'* (Oxford: Pitt Rivers Museum)	
Gathercole, P., Kaeppler, A., & Newton, D.	1979	*Art of the Pacific Islands* (Washington: National Gallery of Art, Washington)	
Gidmark, D.	1988	*The Algonquin Birchbark Canoe* (Princes Risborough: Shire publications)	0852639406
Glover, W.	1994	*Realms of the Pacific* (Belfast: Ulster Museum)	0900761296
Gough, B. M.	1773	*To the Pacific and Arctic with Beechey: The Journal of Lieutenant George Peard on HMS Blossom* (London: Hakluyt)	0521200792
Graham- Stewart, M.	2001	*About Strange Lands and People* (London: Graham-Stewart)	

Author	Year	Title and Publisher	ISBN
Green, R.	1979	'Early Lapita art from Polynesia and Island Melanesia: continuities in ceramic, barkcloth and tattoo' in Mead, S. M. (ed.) *Exploring the Visual Art of Oceania: Australia, Melanesia, Micronesia and Polynesia* (Honolulu: University Press of Hawaii)	
Hackett, R. I. J.	1996	*Art and Religion in Africa* (London: Cassell)	030470424-5
Hauser-Schaublin, B. & Kruger, G.	1998	*James Cook: Gifts and Treasures from the South Seas (the Cook/Forster Collection)* (Gottingen: Prestel)	3791318683
Hiroa, Te Rangi	1944	*Arts & Crafts of the Cook Islands* (Honolulu: Bishop Museum)	
Hiroa, Te Rangi	1958	*The Coming of the Maori* (Wellington: Maori Purposes Fund Board)	
Hitchcock, M.	1991	*Indonesian Textiles* (London: British Museum)	0 71411598 3
Holas, B.	1949	'Vetements d'ecorce battue en Cote d'Ivoire' in *Notes Africaines*; n43:77-80	
Holas, B	1960	*Cultures materielles de la Cote d'Ivoire* (Paris: Presses Universitaires de France)	
Howatt-Krahn, A.	1987	'Conservation – skin and native tanned leather' in *American Indian Art Magazine*, v.12 (2)	
Huffman, K.	1996	' "Up and Over": the opening of the Vanuatu cultural centre complex's new national museum building' in *Pacific Arts*, nos. 13,14: 47-56	
Idiens, D.	1990	*Cook Islands Art* (Princes Risborough: Shire publications)	0747800618
Irwin, A.	1997	'What the witchdoctor ordered' in *The Daily Telegraph*, 2.7.97.	
Johnston, Sir H.	1902	*The Uganda Protectorate* (London)	

Author	Year	Title and Publisher	ISBN
Johnston, V. B.	2003	Notes relating to gudza mats in Zimbabwe (*RAMM archives*)	
Kaeppler, A.	1975	*The Fabrics of Hawaii: Barkcloth* (Leigh-on-Sea: Lewis)	
Kaeppler, A. (ed.)	1978a	*Cook Voyage Artefacts in Leningrad, , Berne and Florence Museums* (Honolulu: Bishop Museum)	091024023
Kaeppler, A.	1978b	*Artificial Curiosities* (Honolulu: Bishop Museum)	0910240248
Kaeppler, A.	2003	'Sculptures of barkcloth and wood from Rapa Nui: symbolic continuities and Polynesian affinities' in *Res* 44: 10-69	0873658450
Kaeppler, A., Kaufmann, C, & Newton, D.	1993 (1997 in Eng.)	*Oceanic Art* (Paris: Citadelles)	0810936933
Kasule, T., Pole, K., & Stein, M.	2003	Finding and buying barkcloth, Kampala, Uganda (RAMM archive)	
Kooijman, S.	1972	*Tapa in Polynesia* (Honolulu: Bishop Museum)	
Kooijman, S.	1977	*Tapa on Moce Island, Fiji: A Traditional Handicraft in a Changing Society* (Leiden: Brill)	
Kooijman, S.	1988	*Polynesian Barkcloth* (Princes Risborough: Shire publications)	0852639430
Leonard, A. & Terrell, J.	1980	*Patterns of Paradise. The styles and significance of bark cloth around the world* (Chicago: Field Museum)	
Lewington, A.	1990	*Plants for people* (London: Natural History Museum and Royal Botanic Gardens Kew)	
Linton, R.	1923	*The Material Culture of the Marquesas Islands* (Honolulu: Bishop Museum)	

Author	Year	Title and Publisher	ISBN
Mack, C. R.	1982	*Polynesian Art at Auction, 1965-1980* (Massachusetts: Mack-Nasser)	0941892018
Matthews, R.	2001	'Arrow-tip poison offers hope for cancer patients' in *Sunday Telegraph*, 13.5.01	
McEwan, C., Barreto, C. & Neves, E.	2001	*Unknown Amazon* (London: British Museum)	071412558X
Melville, H.	1974	*Typee* (London: Folio, reprint)	0460041533
Meyer, A. J. P.	1995	*Oceanic Art* (Cologne: Konemann)	3895080802
Moctezuma, E. M. & Olguin, F. S.	2003	*Aztecs* (London: Royal Academy)	1903973228
More-Gordon, M.	2001	*Hidebound by tradition* (Devon Life, Feb 2001)	
Neich, R. & Pendergrast, M.	1997	*Traditional Tapa textiles of the Pacific* (London: Thames & Hudson)	0500279896
Newton, D. (ed.)	1999	*Arts of the South Seas* (Geneva: Barbier Mueller Museum/Prestel)	3791320920
Nzita, R. & Mbaga, N.	1993	*Peoples and Cultures of Uganda* (Kampala: Fountain)	9970020315
O'Hanlon, M.	1993	*Paradise: Portraying the New Guinea Highlands* (London: British Museum)	0714125091
Ohlsen, B. & Durrans, B.	1994	*Ainu Material Culture from the Notes of N. G. Munro,* (London: British Museum, Occ Pap 96)	0861590961
Phelps, S.	1976	*Art & Artefacts of the Pacific, Africa and the Americas* (London: Christies)	0091250005
Picton, J.	1980	'Women's weaving: the Manufacture and Use of Textiles among the Igbirra People of Nigeria' in Idiens, D. & Ponting, K. G. (eds.) *Textiles of Africa* (Bath: Pasold)	0903859084

Author	Year	Title and Publisher	ISBN
Picton, J. & Mack, J.	1979	*African Textiles* (London: British Museum)	0714115525
Pole, L.	2001	'Barkcloth in Ghana' in Wright, M. M. (ed.) *Barkcloth: Aspects of preparation, use, deterioration, conservation and display* (London: Archetype, London)	1873132824
Prance, G. T. & A. E.	1993	*Bark* (Portland, Oregon)	0881922625
Pritchard, M. J.	1984	*Siapo: Bark cloth art of Samoa* (American Samoa: Council on Culture, Arts and Humanities)	
Rahme, L. & Hartman, D.	1998	*Preparation and Tanning by Traditional Methods* (New York: Caber Press)	
Reynolds, B.	1968	*Material Culture of the Peoples of the Gwembe Valley* (Manchester: Manchester University)	
Robertson, G.	1973	*The Discovery of Tahiti* (London: Folio)	046004141X
Roscoe, J.	1965	*The Baganda* (London: Cass)	
Roth, J. & Hooper, S.	1990	*Fiji Journals of Baron Anatole von Hugel* (Cambridge/Fiji Museum)	982208000
Sayce, R. U.	1933	*Primitive Arts & Crafts* (Cambridge: Cambridge University)	
Sayer, C.	1993	*Arts & Crafts of Mexico* (London: Thames & Hudson)	
Sieber, R.	1972	*African Textiles and Decorative Arts* (New York: Museum of Modern Art)	0870702270
Shaw, A.	1787	*A Catalogue of the different specimens of cloth collected on the three voyages of Captain Cook* (London: Shaw)	
Shepherd, S.	2003	*Seeds of Fortune* (London: Bloomsbury)	07475600668

Author	Year	Title and Publisher	ISBN
Smith, J.	1882	*Dictionary of economic plants* (London: Macmillan & Co)	
Starzecka, D. & Cranstone, B.	1974	*The Solomon Islanders* (London: British Museum)	071411358X
Starzecka, D.	1996	*Maori Art & Culture* (London: British Museum)	0714125245
Storch, P. S.	1987	'Curatorial care and handling of skin materials: Part II Semi-tanned objects', *Conservation Notes no.18.2*	
Steward, J. H. & Faron, L. C.	1959	*Native Peoples of South America* (New York: McGraw Hill)	
Stewart, H.	1984	*Cedar: Tree of life to the Northwest Coast Indians* (Vancouver: University of British Columbia)	
Strathern, A. & M.	1971	*Self Decoration in Mount Hagen* (London, Duckworth)	071560516
Suggs, R.	1960	*Island Civilisations of Polynesia* (New York: Mentor)	
Thomas, N.	1995	*Oceanic Art* (London: Thames & Hudson)	0500202818
Turnbull, C.	1961	*The Forest People* (London: Book Club Associates)	
Turner, N. J.	1998	*Plant Technology of first peoples in British Columbia* (Vancouver: University of British Columbia)	0774806877
Vaillant, G. C.	1950	*The Aztecs of Mexico* (London: Penguin Books)	
Von Hagen, V. W.	1957	*The Ancient Sun Kingdoms of the Americas* (New York: World Publishing Co.)	
Waite, D. B.	1987	*Artefacts from the Solomon Islands* in the Julius L. Brenchley Collection (London: British Museum)	01714115703
Welsch, R. L. (ed.)	1998	*An American Anthropologist in Melanesia* (Honolulu: U. Hawaii Press)	0824816447